ECO DESIGN

ENVIRONMENTALLY SOUND PACKAGING AND GRAPHIC DESIGN

First published in the United States of America by:
Rockport Publishers, Inc.
146 Granite Street
Rockport, Massachusetts 01966
Telephone: (508) 546-9590
Fax: (508) 546-7141

Distributed to the book trade and art trade in the U.S. by:
North Light, an imprint of
F & W Publications
1507 Dana Avenue
Cincinnati, Ohio 45207
Telephone: (513) 531-2222

Other Distribution by:
Rockport Publishers, Inc.
Rockport, Massachusetts 01966

ISBN 1-56496-083-8

10 9 8 7 6 5 4 3 2 1

Art Director: Laura Herrmann
Design Firm: Brand Design Company
Cover Photograph: Carlos Alejandro

Printed in China

ECO DESIGN

ENVIRONMENTALLY SOUND PACKAGING AND GRAPHIC DESIGN

Rockport Publishers, Inc.
Rockport, Massachusetts

TABLE OF CONTENTS

There is really no excuse today for not combining design innovation with concern for the environment. Although there is still plenty of room for improvement in print production techniques and in the manufacturing of materials we use, the choices that allow designers to "do the right thing" are there.

Environmentally sound design should go beyond simply using recycled paper and soy-based inks; it should begin long before these choices are made. At the conceptual stage of design development we need to consider the impact that our work will have on the Earth. How can we reduce source materials without sacrificing visual impact? Can a second use for our piece keep it from the waste stream while making the design message live on? Is it possible to solve a client's marketing problem and reduce the number of printed pieces they use to do so? And how can we, as skilled communicators, get the message out to the general public about the need to protect our environment? These are some of the questions that we should be asking ourselves daily as we go about the business of creating design.

Design innovation and environmental concern are not mutually exclusive. A design cannot be considered "best" unless its environmental impact has been considered and dealt with in the most innovative way. Every design competition should, as this one does, have the designer's concern for the world we live in as one of its criteria for excellence.

-Joseph Duffy
Duffy Design Group

Save me, please. I'm here.

Environmental concern as we know it today is more than a state of mind—it has become a marketing boon for everything from paper companies to automobile manufacturers. But what is environmentally sound graphic design? Is it scanning brown Kraft, printing it four color process on 10% recycled-content white gloss and mailing a million pieces with an expected response rate of three percent? Or is it peeling the bark off of dead trees and scratching messages on it with charcoal pencil? Well, hopefully it's somewhere between the two.

In this age of environmental concern, designers are faced with an increasing ethical dilemma: the key to true environmental concern eats away at the very core of our means of making a living. Does a client really need to print 50,000 annual reports, or can he get by with 10,000. Can you make do with 24 pages instead of 36—just crowd all of that information on fewer pages, right? When you're giving marketing advice, are you going to tell your client that he probably shouldn't print that next piece because it's really going to add a lot of tonnage to the landfill?

It's a tough dilemma. If all designers made a consistent effort toward designing with the environment in mind, it would have a substantial positive impact on our fragile ecology. Good planning, great design, and self-education about the environmental issues surrounding the graphics industry are effective ways to ease the burden on our over-taxed environment.

In his forward to this book, Joseph Duffy really hits the nail on the head—true environmental concern must come in the early conceptual stages of graphic design. We hope that this book gives you some ideas on how to keep Mother Earth in mind when developing your next piece.

R.E.M. Post Office Box 8032
ATHENS, GEORGIA 30603

R.E.M.

ATHENS GEORGIA 30603 POST OFFICE BOX 8032

usa

R.E.M.
POST BOX 8032
ATHENS
GA. 30603 USA

INDEPENDENT PROJECT PRESS

Independent Project Press is a small letterpress-based printer in Arizona, owned and operated by Bruce and Karen Licher.

The following pieces are great examples of efficient use of materials and Old World letterpress printing techniques. We dedicated a small section of this book to the work of Independent Project Press because of their unique and effective approach to environmentally sound graphic design and production.

All of the pieces in this section are printed on industrial-grade papers and packaging materials with a high recycled content. The very nature of letterpress printing is also environmentally sound because it often requires less raw material to create the actual printing plates. For example, hand-set type eliminates the need for chemicals used to burn offset printing plates and to develop film negatives. Type set in lead can also be completely recycled—when the print job is done, the type is simply melted for the next project.

Various promotional pieces (for the rock group R.E.M.) by Bruce Licher of Independent Project Press

Mai Pen Rai CD Package

Design Firm
Independent Project Press

Art Director/Designer
Bruce Licher

Client
4.A.D. Records

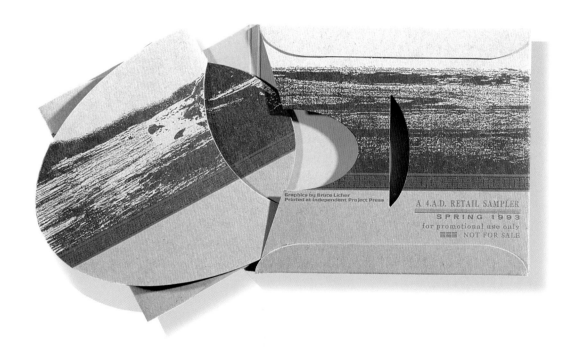

Red Temple Spirits – "New Land"
7 inch Single Cover

Design Firm
Independent Project Press

Art Director/Designer
Bruce Licher

Client
Independent Project Records

Red Temple Spirits – "New Land"
7 inch Single Cover

Design Firm
Independent Project Press

Art Director/Designer
Bruce Licher

Client
Independent Project Records

If one advances confidently in the direction of his dreams,
and endeavors to live the life that he has imagined,
he will meet with a success unexpected in common hours.

-- *Henry David Thoreau*

Designed and printed by Karen & Bruce Licher at
INDEPENDENT PROJECT PRESS

**R.E.M. Christmas Card
& Holiday Stayflat**

Design Firm
Independent Project Press

Art Director/Designers
Karen & Bruce Licher

Illustrator
Karen Licher

Client
R.E.M./Athens, Ltd.

**Independent Project Press
Portfolio Cover**
(facing page)

Design Firm
Independent Project Press

Art Director/Designers
Karen and Bruce Licher

Illustrator
Karen Licher

The leaf was printed from an
actual leaf; mounted on
masonite and run through the
press. Approximately 125
impressions were made before
the leaf began to deteriorate.

INDEPENDENT
PROJECT  PRESS

544 MATEO STREET

LOS ANGELES
90013

"Insomnia, Vol. 1"
CD Package

Design Firm
Independent Project Press

Art Director/Designer
Bruce Licher

Client
We Never Sleep

A double CD package produced for a compilation CD of early alternative industrial music.

R.E.M. Holiday Fan Club
Single Cover
"Where's Captain Kirk?"

Design Firm
Independent Project Press

Art Director/Designer
Bruce Licher

Client
R.E.M./Athens, Ltd.

R.E.M. Holiday Fan Club
Single Cover
"Baby Baby"

Design Firm
Independent Project Press

Art Director/Designer
Bruce Licher

Client
R.E.M./Athens, Ltd.

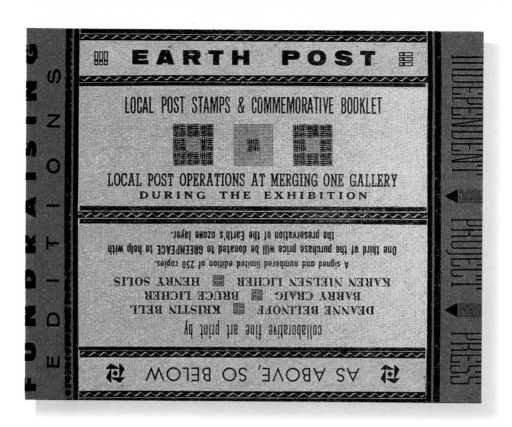

EARTH POST

LOCAL POST STAMPS & COMMEMORATIVE BOOKLET

LOCAL POST OPERATIONS AT MERGING ONE GALLERY
DURING THE EXHIBITION

the preservation of the Earth's ozone layer.
One third of the purchase price will be donated to GREENPEACE to help with
A signed and numbered limited edition of 250 copies.

KAREN NIELSEN LICHER ▦ HENRY SOLIS
BARRY CRAIG ▦ BRUCE LICHER
DEANNE BELINOFF ▦ KRISTIN BELL
collaborative fine art print by

AS ABOVE, SO BELOW

FUNDRAISING EDITIONS

INDEPENDENT PROJECT PRESS

**Earth Day Fundraising
Editions Postcard**

Design Firm
Independent Project Press

Art Director/Designer
Bruce Licher

Copy
Bruce and Karen Licher

**One of three postcards
mailed in a glassine
envelope announcing the
"Landmarks" Earth Day
exhibit at Merging One
Gallery in Santa Monica, CA.**

Earth Post Stamp Booklet

Design Firm
Independent Project Press

Art Director/Designer
Bruce Licher

Copy
Bruce Licher

**This souvenir stamp booklet
was for an Earth Day art
exhibit. Two dollars from
each booklet sold was
donated to Greenpeace
and the Cosanti Foundation.**

BOOKLET OF 40
EARTH POST STAMPS
LOCAL POST COMMEMORATIVES
FOR THE BENEFIT OF
GREENPEACE & THE COSANTI FOUNDATION

Independent Project Shop Bag

Design Firm
Independent Project Press

Art Director/Designer
Bruce Licher

Client
The Independent Project Shop

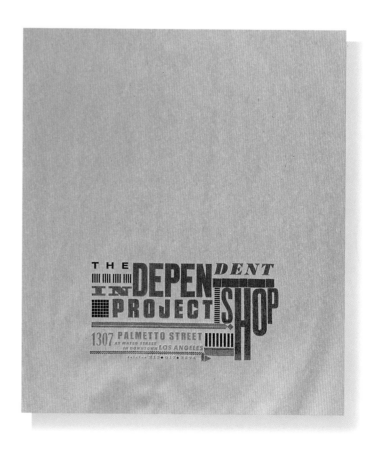

THE INDEPENDENT PROJECT SHOP
1307 PALMETTO STREET
AT MATEO STREET
IN DOWNTOWN LOS ANGELES

**Independent Project
10th Anniversary
Mail Order Catalog Cover**

Design Firm
Independent Project Press

Art Director/Designer
Bruce Licher

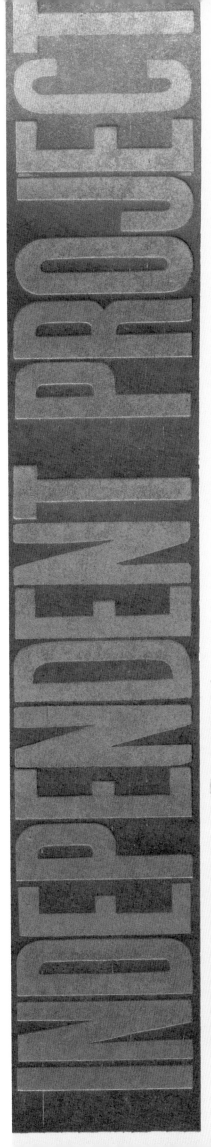

TENTH ANNIVERSARY
MAILORDER
CATALOG

OF ALL ITEMS CURRENTLY AVAILABLE FROM

INDEPENDENT PROJECT
RECORDS & PRESS

* ✳ PHONOGRAPH RECORDS
* ✳ CDS & CASSETTES
* ✳ PRINTED EPHEMERA

✶ PRICE: TWO DOLLARS ✶

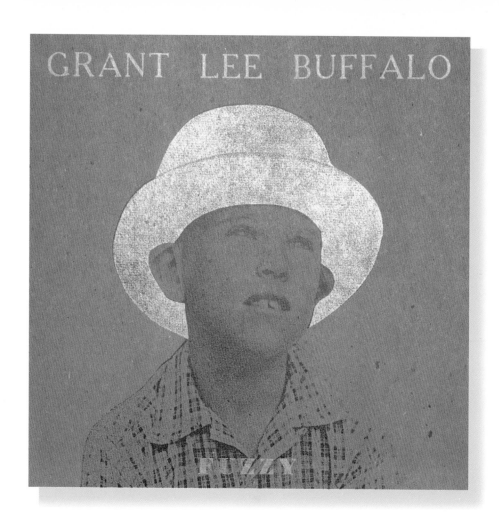

Grant Lee Buffalo–"Fuzzy"
7 inch Single Cover

Design Firm
Independent Project Press

Art Director
Bruce Licher/Grant Lee Phillips

Designer
Bruce Licher

Photographer
Kimberly Wright

Client
Singles Only Label

Buffalo Tom–"Soda Jerk"
7 inch Single Cover

Design Firm
Independent Project Press

Art Director
Bruce Licher/Bob Hamilton

Designer
Bruce Licher

Photographer
Allen Penn

Client
Atlantic Records

**Independent Project Press
Typeface Catalog**

Design Firm
Independent Project Press

Art Directors/Designers
Karen and Bruce Licher

INDEPENDENT PROJECT PRESS

TYPEFACES
AND
ORNAMENTS

SECOND EDITION

**544 MATEO STREET
LOS ANGELES ◈ CALIF. 90013**

PHONE & FAX:

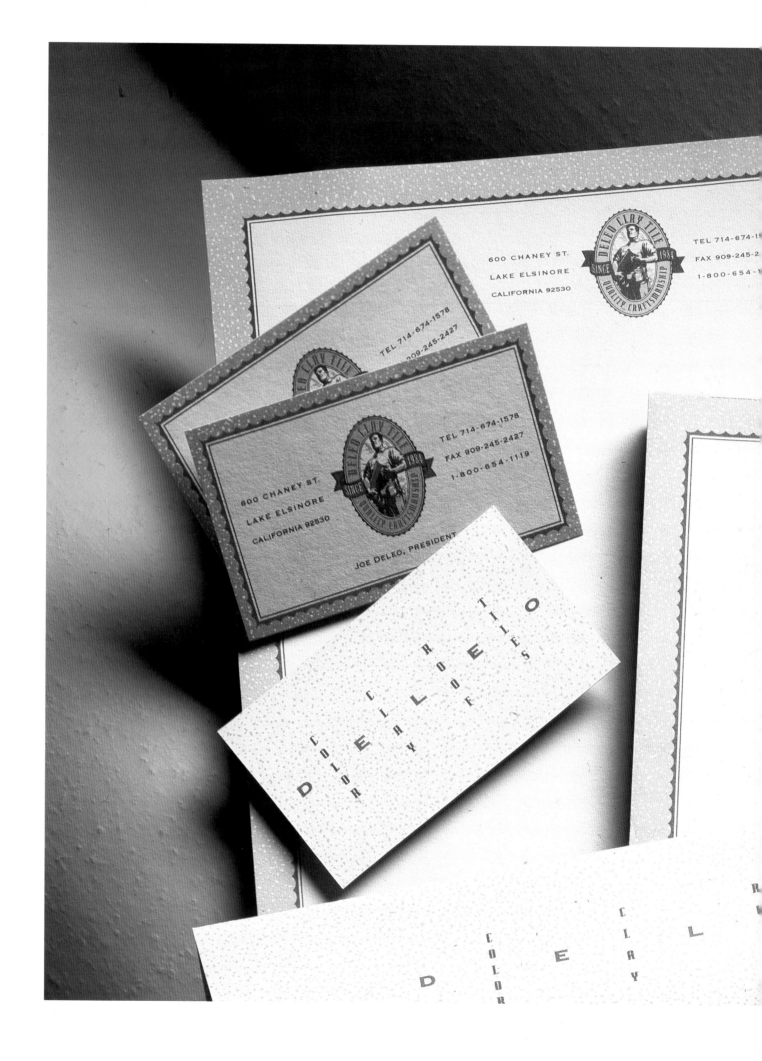

IDENTITY

Businesses go through mounds of letterhead, envelopes, and business cards every year, adding tons of paper to the waste stream. By using environmentally sound materials and production techniques, designers can have a substantial impact on the environment while enhancing a corporation's public image.

Deleo Identity Systems

Design Firm
Mires Design, Inc.

Art Director
José Serrano

Designer
José Serrano

Photographer
Chris Wimpey

Client
Deleo Clay Tile Company

The whole identity system is based on recycling and reusing; using natural materials that the Earth provides. All items were printed on recycled French Speckletone.

Deleo Letterhead System
(facing page)

Design Firm
Mires Design, Inc.

Art Director
José Serrano

Designer
José Serrano

Illustrator
Nancy Stahl

Client
Deleo Clay Tile Company

Printer
Bordeaux Printers

Printed in three PMS colors on recycled Speckletone Kraft

Deleo Placard

Design Firm
Mires Design, Inc.

Art Director
José Serrano

Designer
José Serrano

Illustrator
Nancy Stahl

Client
Deleo Clay Tile Company

Printer
Bordeaux Printers

Printed in two PMS colors and one thermography on recycled French Speckletone Kraft.

Burton Identity

Design Firm
Jager Di Paola Kemp Design

Art Director
Michael Jager, David Covell

Designer
David Covell

Client
Burton Snowboards

Printer
Queen City Printer

The stationery uses recycled Neenah Environment Desert Storm, which contains 15% post-consumer waste made up of return mail and office waste.

Burton Shopping Bags

Design Firm
Jager Di Paola Kemp Design

Art Director
Michael Jager, David Covell

Designer
David Covell

Client
Burton Snowboards

Printed on recycled brown Kraft.

Self-Promotional Flyer

All Design/Illustration
J. Otto Seibold

Client
Newsweek

This piece was output on
recycled French Dur-O-Tone
Butcher on an Iris dye-
sublimation color printer.

Mailing Envelope

All Design/Illustration
J. Otto Seibold

Created by re-using envelopes
with bold, strong copy that
were found in the garbage.
The labels are laser-printed
as needed, eliminating waste.

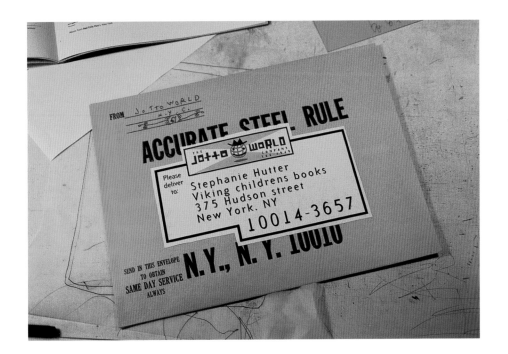

Microsoft Mail Invitation

Design Firm
The Leonhardt Group

Art Director
Ross Hogin

Photographer
Jon Cannell

Illustrator
Jon Cannell, George Cheney

Client
Microsoft

Copywriter
Jeff Fraga

Printer
Heath

Production/Printing
**Offset, Lithography,
and Screen Printing**

The paper for this piece is
89% recycled with 19% post-
consumer waste and is acid
free. It is a self mailer with
a logo sticker, eliminating
the need for an envelope.

Self-Promotional Card

All Design/Illustration
J. Otto Seibold

Printer
Okeanos Press

This busy, modern design
uses an old-fashioned
2-color printing technique
on recycled paper.

RadioActive Ink

Design Firm
Werner Design Werks

All Design/Illustration
Sharon Werner

Client
Radioactive Ink

Copy
Radioactive Ink

Printer
**Torgerson Printing,
Quick Print, Custom Color**

Production/Printing
Letterpress, Offset

The design began in a paper
warehouse where Werner
Design Werks found leftover
letterhead slated to be discarded. The silver on the back
of the letterhead was a bonus;
it gave the identity system an
immediate presence without
the expense of printing a new
design. The rest of the identity
package was designed around
the letterhead, using a comple-
mentary recycled paper stock.
Printing was kept to a minimum, stickers were used
for added color and texture.

Postcards/Business Card

Design Firm
John Gambell Graphic Design

Designer
John Gambell

Production/Printing
Rubber Stamp, Engraving

In the course of their work, John Gambell Graphic Design generates small pieces of high quality colored cover stock, which are often unacceptable to recyclers.

The firm designed a large rubber stamp to quickly convert this scrap into colorful postcards, which are used for informal correspondence with clients and suppliers.

Acme Rubber Stamp Stationery

Design Firm
Peterson & Company

Art Director
Bryan L. Peterson

Designer
Bryan L. Peterson, Dave Eliason

Client
Acme Rubber Stamp

Printer
Monarch Press

This stationery is 100% recyclable paper, which complements the industrial location of the stamp manufacturer. Because the company logo is rubber stamped, it functions not only as corporate identity, but also as an example of what the company produces.

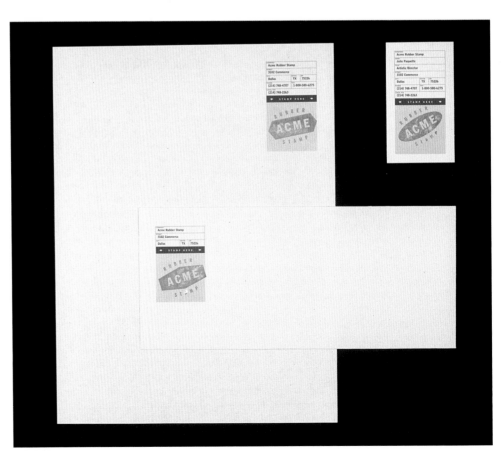

Art Rep
Identity Package

Design Firm
Werner Design Werks

All Design/Illustration
Sharon Werner

Client
Joanie Bernstein

Printer
Torgerson Printing,
Print Craft, Inc., Duffy Paper

Production/Printing
Offset, Letterpress, Flexo

For this project, end cut papers from other jobs were purchased from a warehouse. The letterhead stock is actually paper that is usually used to wrap reams of other paper, the envelope is florist wrap, and the business card is stock that has been on the floor so long it has yellowed on the edges (an added plus). The printed tape holds the identity together. Printing on the envelope was eliminated by adding the tape. Colors were kept to a minimum to keep the package affordable.

31

Art Dreko Hang Tags

Design Firm
Mires Design, Inc.

Art Director/Designer
Scott Mires

Illustrator
Gerald Bustamante

Client
Art Dreko

Production/Printing
Offset on recycled stock

Art Dreko is a decorative, functional art firm that creatively reuses personal, household, and industrial waste. These hang tags use recycled paper and were designed to reflect the recycled elements of the Art Dreko pieces.

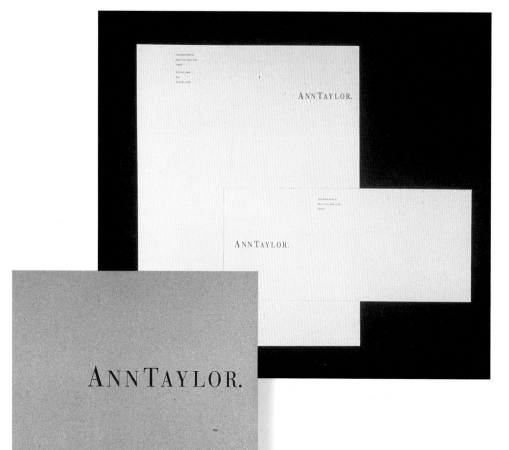

Ann Taylor Identity Package

Design Firm
Cato Gobé & Associates

Creative Director
Marc Gobé

Art Director
Peter Levine

Designer
Peter Levine

Photographer
J.R. Durand

Client
Ann Taylor

Copy
Cato Gobé & Associates

Recycled materials are used in all Ann Taylor identity and packaging materials.

Dewitt Kendall Letterhead

Design Firm/Art Director
Dewitt Kendall

Printer
Amos Kennedy & Sons

Production/Printing
Letterpress

This letterhead campaign is about contrasts. Very expensive Indian paper, handmade from recycled cotton rags and rice husks, is used in combination with two of the cheapest and most ubiquitous materials around…industrial chipboard and brown Kraft paper. It is also important to note that the only way to print all three of these drastically different materials the same way involved recycling an old technology…Letterpress.

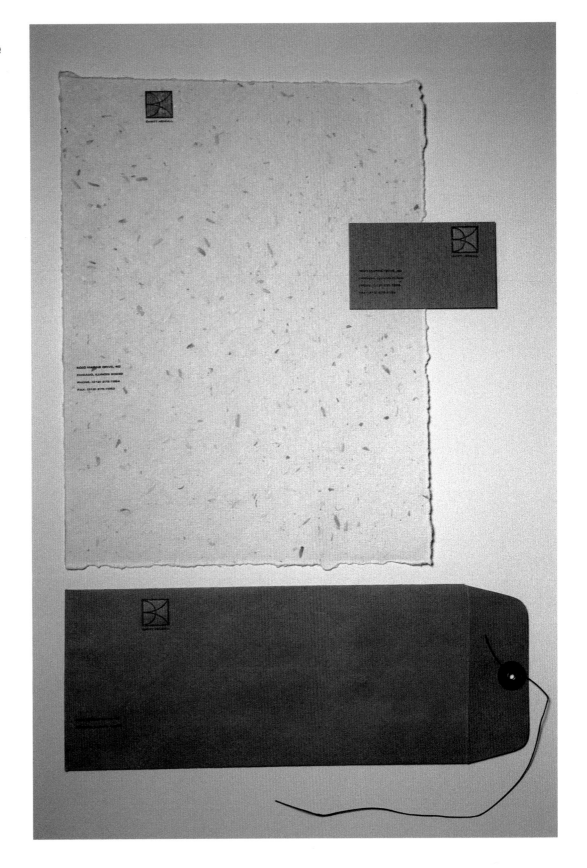

Daven Film & Video Stationery

Design Firm
Earl Gee Design

Art Director/Designer/Illustrator
Earl Gee

Client
Daven Film & Video

Printer
Multi-Image Press

The recycled paper used on this identity system created a low-tech, craft-oriented feel for a very high-tech industry.

Community Partnership of Santa Clara County Stationery

Design Firm
Earl Gee Design

Art Director/Designer/Illustrator
Fani Chung

Client
Community Partnership of Santa Clara County

Printer
Express Quality Printing

The recycled paper was a natural choice for this non-profit organization dedicated to "linking people and ideas to find contemporary solutions" to build better communities.

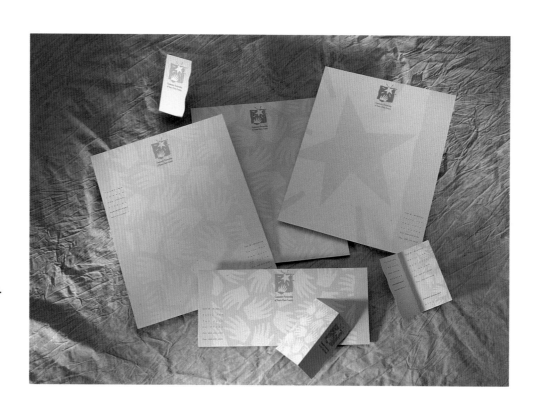

**Gare du Vin Wine List
and Identity Materials**

Design Firm
Design House Consultants

Art Director
Chris Lower

Designer
Andrew Cross

Photographer
Paul Dunn

Illustrator
Delores Fairman

Client
Allied-Lyons—Victoria Wine

Natural recycled materials
were used throughout this
identity and promotional
program to add simple,
authentic appeal.

PACKAGING

Packaging design offers a
wide range of multi-dimensional
opportunities for using environ-
mentally-sound materials.
This section shows the unique
use of packing materials and
alternate media to create eye-
catching and environmentally-
friendly packaging.

K. D. Lang—"Ingénue"
Special CD Package

Design Firm
Warner Bros. Records

Art Director
Jeri Heiden

Designer
Jeri Heiden, Greg Ross

Photographer
Glen Erler

Client
Warner Bros./Sire

Printer
Westland Graphics, Ivy Hill

All packaging materials used on Warner Brothers' CDs are recycled: recycled plastic for jewel cases and trays, and recycled paper for booklets. In this case, K.D. Lang wanted an additional outer package made of recycled materials to create the look and feel of a gift wrap. E-flute cardboard is used for the wrap and recycled paper for the belly band. Printing was kept to a bare minimum—one color, "Ingénue Green."

**Gap Warehouse
Denim Labeling System**

Design Firm
Gap Advertising

Creative Director
Maggie Gross

Designer
Siras Greiner

Illustrator
Alan Disparte

Client
Gap Warehouse

Copy
Anne Buhl

Gap Advertising uses paper
with 50% recycled content,
at least 10% of which is post-
consumer waste.

Prince Racket Packaging

Design Firm
One World Solutions Inc.

Art Director
Brent Robertson

Designer
Dane Sorenson

Client
Prince Manufacturing, Inc.

Printer
Adds Graphics

Printing Techniques
Silkscreen

Minimal one-color screen printing and recycled brown wrap for the rackets make this an attractive yet environmentally sound alternative to conventional packaging.

**Indiana Popping Corn
Packaging**

Design Firm
Horner/Rundquist, Inc.

Art Director
Julie Horner, Pete Rundquist

Designer
Julie Horner, Brian Turner

Illustrator
Ernie Boetz

Client
Americorn, Inc.

Copy
Julie Horner, Pete Rundquist

Printer
**American Packaging and
Oakes Carton Company**

Production/Printing
3-color Flexo

Americorn, Inc. is owned and operated by several generations of an American Indian farming family. They wanted to stress the closeness they felt with nature and their crop by using natural-colored and recycled materials. This package is quite a contrast with other corporations' impersonal popcorn packaging.

Mohawk Paper Packaging

Design Firm
Pentagram Design/NY

Art Director
Michael Bierut

Designer
Lisa Cerveny

Client
Mohawk Paper Mills, Inc.

Breaking the tradition of wrapping paper in white stock, Mohawk adopted an environmental approach: They package their recycled paper in Kraft boxes and ream wrap, both printed in one color.

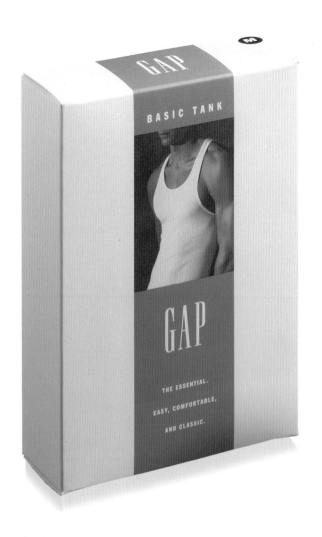

Gap Women's and Men's Underwear Packaging

Design Firm
Gap Advertising

Creative Director
Maggie Gross

Designer
Siras Greiner

Photographer
David Michalek

Illustrator
An-Ching Chang

Client
Gap

Copywriter
Lisa Salmon

Print Production Manager
Marlene Braga

Printer
Queens Group

This package uses recycled white packaging board with at least 10% post-consumer waste and is printed with soy-based inks.

Gap Denim Press Kit

Design Firm
Gap Advertising

Art Director
Doug Lloyd

Creative Director
Maggie Gross

Designer
Roz Romney

Client
Gap Public Relations

Copy
Timothy Cohrs

The boxes for these press kits are unprinted brown fluted-cardboard, one of the most recyclable packaging materials.

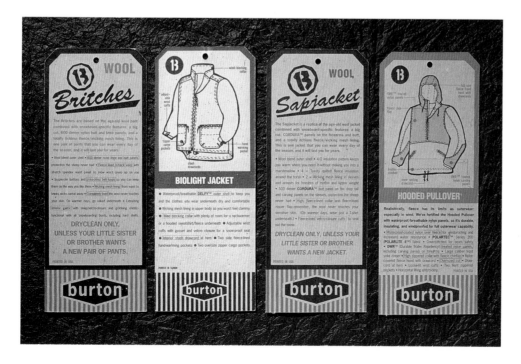

Burton Hangtags

Design Firm
Jager Di Paola Kemp Design

Art Director
Michael Jager, David Covell

Designer
Dan Sharp

Client
Burton Snowboards

Printer
Queen City Printers

Printed on recycled cover stock containing at least 25% post-consumer waste.

Converse Shoe Boxes

Design Firm
Clifford Selbert Design

Design Team
Melanie Lowe

Photographer
Francine Zaslow

Client
Converse, Inc.

These boxes are constructed of 100% recyclable board and are printed in one color.

Lush "Spooky" Velvet CD Pak

Design Firm
V23/4AD Records

Art Director
Jeff Gold, Vaughan Oliver

Designer
Jeff Gold, Vaughan Oliver

Photographer
Jim Friedman

Client
Reprise/4AD Records

Printer
AGI, Ivy Hill

This project involved a different kind of recycling. Warner Brothers Records bought enough blue velvet to cover 10,000 special CD packages. Then, at the last minute, the artist chose something else—leaving the company in the lurch with an awful lot of blue velvet. A few months later, Warner Brothers' art director was speaking to the band Lush, who wanted to do a special, limited edition package. He made the connection between velvet and Lush, and the band loved the idea.

Summit Packaging

Design Firm
Cato Gobé & Associates

Creative Director
Marc Gobé

Art Director
Bill Hovard

Designer
John Duffy

Client
Bath & Body Works

Copywriter
Cato Gobé & Associates

Printer
Arco

Production/Printing
Offset, recycled Kraft board

Simple packaging lets the details of Summit, a line of men's grooming products from Bath & Body Works, shine. The design was inspired by natural materials—straw, wood, even potatoes—indigenous to the American heartlands, as well as handforged tools, such as one might find on a farmer's workbench. Recycled brown Kraft is used for all of the packaging materials.

**Hush Puppies Packaging
and POP Materials**

Design Firm
Fitch Inc.

Art Director
Jamie Alexander

Designer
Paul Westrick

Photographer
Mark Steele, Fitch, Inc.

Client
**Hush Puppies, Division of
Wolverine Worldwide**

Recycled stocks were used in
the boxes as well as in the
shopping bags, which promote
the use of paper over plastic.

**Luveon
Big Heart Soap Pack**

Design Firm
**Kan Tài-keung Design
& Associates, Ltd.**

Art Director
Kan Tài-keung

Designer
Kan Tài-keung

Client
Lutex Co. Ltd.

The Heart Soap Pack uses recycled fluted Kraft board and recycled paper for the labels.

**Holden & Co. Holiday
Gift Wrap Package**

Design Firm
Holden & Co.

Designer
Cathe Holden

Client
Holden & Co.

Printer
**ColorWise Printing &
Lithography**

Production/Printing
**Metallic inks, all
printed two times.**

**This piece was designed to
be reused by the recipient.
Recycled paper and twine gives
it a friendly, "recycled" look.**

The Four Horsemen
Jean Pocket Package

Design Firm
American Recordings

Designer
Alan Forbes (Label)

Client
American Recordings

The jean pocket package fit the image of this Southern Rock band. The package is made from denim from discarded blue jeans.

Greenscreen

Design Firm
Rigelhaupt Design

Art Director/Designer
Gail Rigelhaupt

Photographer
Norbert Schoener

Client
Greenscreen International

Copy
Lauren & James Benjamin

Printer
Rose City Paper

Production/Printing
Offset Printing

The packaging uses only
recycled board to convey
the company's commitment to
recycling and the environment.
A competing product is
packaged in heavy plastic
blister packs.

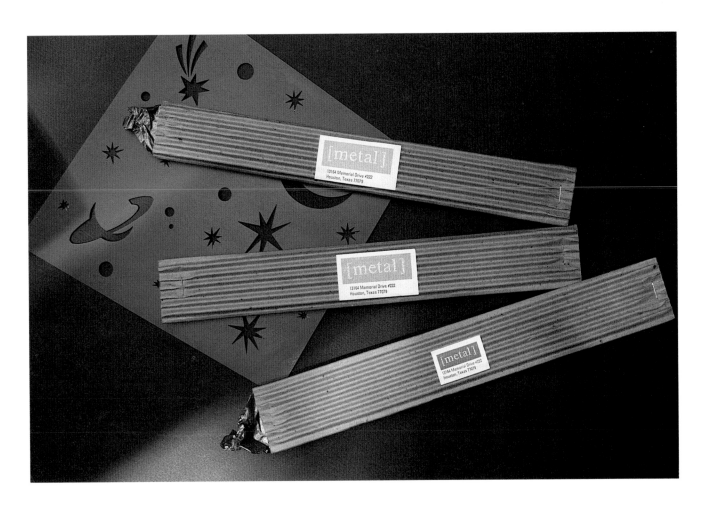

Letter Opener Packaging

Design Firm
Peat Jariya Design

Art Director/Designer
Peat Jariya

Client
[Metal] Studio Corp.

Printer
Boehm Inc.

This letter opener packaging is made of recycled corrugated boards stapled shut on both ends for economy, ease of distribution, rustic appeal, and function. The labels are printed in one-color on recycled paper.

Cornerstone Holiday Promotion

Design Firm
Cornerstone

Art Director
Keith Steimel

Illustrator
Keith Steimel

Copy
Keith Steimel

These self-mailers were made entirely of recycled paper products and included a live Douglas Fir sapling to be planted by the recipient. Each piece was printed on a laser printer.

Greenpeace—"Alternative NRG"

Design Firm
Hollywood Records

Art Director
**Maria DeGrassi-Colosimo/
Lee Liebe**

Designer
**Maria DeGrassi-Colosimo/
Jamile Mafi**

Photographer
**Maria DeGrassi-Colosimo
(cover/computer montage)**

Client
Hollywood Records/Greenpeace

Printer
Shorewood (Canada)

All of the stock used for this
packaging is recycled and is
bleached with a chlorine-free
process. All the inks used are
vegetable/soy oil-based.

Brian May—"Driven By You"

Design Firm
Hollywood Records

Art Director
Maria DeGrassi-Colosimo

Designer
Maria DeGrassi-Colosimo

Photographer
**Richard Gray (inside)
Maria DeGrassi-Colosimo
(cover/photo montage)**

Client
Hollywood Records

Printer
AGI

Box Design
AGI

This compact disc package
is environmentally sound by
virtue of its intricate construc-
tion; the package lends itself
to being kept forever, instead
of being thrown away.

D.D. Wood—"Louie Cooper"

Design Firm
Hollywood Records

Art Director
Maria DeGrassi-Colosimo

Designer
Maria DeGrassi-Colosimo

Photographer
Reisig & Taylor (cover)
James Colosimo (inside)

Client
Hollywood Records

Printer
Modern Album

This minimalist packaging
is made completely of
recyclable paperboard
and contains no plastics.

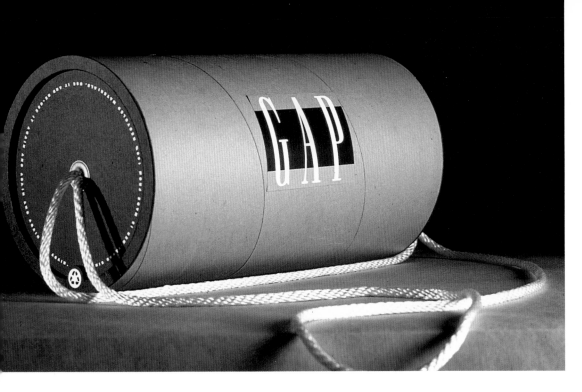

Proposed GAP Shoe Packaging

Design Firm
Tharp Did It

Designer
Rick Tharp

Client
The Gap

Copywriter
Rick Tharp

This package is not only made from 100% recycled materials but, after the purchase, it is also 100% reusable: The tube doubles as a tote bag when a rope is strung though both ends.

Deleo Clay Tile Packaging

Design Firm
Mires Design, Inc.

All Design
José Serrano

Illustrator
Tracy Sabin

Client
Deleo Clay Tile Company

Copywriter
Kelly Smothermon

Printer
Rush Press

These labels are printed in two colors on recycled paper and then laminated to recycled Kraft board.

Christmas Card Packaging

Designer
**Lynn Trickett, Brian Webb,
Andrew Thomas**

Client
WH Smith

WH Smith reinvents the traditional methods of gift wrapping a box by using such environmentally friendly materials as recycled paper and gardeners' string.

LeBoulanger Shopping Bags

Design Firm
Tharp Did It

Art Director
Rick Tharp

Designer
Rick Tharp and Jean Mogannam

Illustrator
Rick Tharp

Client
LeBoulanger Bakeries

The bags are printed with flexography on recycled brown Kraft.

Intentionally Blank

Design Firm
Design Guys

Art Director
Steven Sikora

Designer
Steven Sikora, Bruce Macindoe

Copy
Steven Sikora

Printer
Cold Side, Quick Print

This seemingly blank product and recycled Kraft paper is a statement for those who are forever asked and expected to be clever, full of marketable gimmicks, phrases, and trends.

Class 5 Packaging & Hangtag

Design Firm
Alternatives

Art Director
Mark Koch

Designer
Kevin Yates

The design objective was to produce this package using as little glue and paper as possible. Instead of following the standard practice of gluing printed paper to the box, the graphics were printed directly on the chipboard, saving materials, extra processes, and expense.

**Dai-ichi Hotel Tokyo
Amenity Bottles**

Design Firm
UCI Inc.

Art Director
Ryo Urano

Designers
Chris Kehlor, Kay Clark

Photographer
Raymond Wong

Client
Dai-ichi Hotel, Ltd.

Fabricator
**Pelican Soap Co., Ltd. and
Suntube Co., Ltd.**

This packaging is environmentally sound in a very technical way. A plastic know as P.E.T. (Polyethylene-Terephthalate) was used because it has a low combustion point and doesn't emit toxic gas when burned, making it easy and safe to incinerate.

**Squeeze—"Play"
Special CD Package**

Design Firm
Warner Bros. Records

Art Director
Jeff Gold, Kim Champagne

Designer
Kim Champagne

Photographer
Enrique Badulescu

Client
Reprise Records

Printer
Ivy Hill

This special package reuses old corrugated boxes which are labeled with recycled paper. The contents of the box are made entirely of organic materials except for the CD itself.

Carnegie Libraries
Restoration & Expansion

Design Firm
DeWitt Kendall

Art Director
DeWitt Kendall

Client
Frye Gillan Molinaro, Ltd.

Copy
Lonn Frye

Printer
Omni Printing, Inc./
Intermark 7

"Carnegie Libraries" arose out of an effort to break a great number of rules which govern the traditionally dry category of trade and reference books. Because the book asks municipalities to recycle their Carnegie Libraries, recycled materials were an integral part of the project. Nearly all the elements used in the book are recycled materials, down to scrap yard copper sheets used for the silk screened title tags, and leather cord purchased from an army surplus outlet. The body text paper is Cross Pointe Genesis (Bone) which is made from 100% de-inked fiber, containing a minimum of 15% post-consumer waste. The cover is Simpson Gainsborough, also a recycled stock.

**Paul Westerberg—"14 Songs"
Special Package**

Design Firm
Warner Bros. Records

Art Director
Kim Champagne, Jeff Gold

Designer
**Kim Champagne (Booklet),
Jean Krikorian**

Photographer
**Frank Ockenfels,
Kim Champagne**

Concept and Design
**Paul Westerberg,
Kim Champagne**

Client
Reprise/Sire Records

Printer
Ivy Hill

The entire book is printed in one color. The cover is plain pressboard with no lamination or fabric cover, making it completely biodegradable.

Hanson's Maple Syrup

Design Firm
Hanson Associates, Inc.

Art Director
Gil Hanson

Designer
Christy Verna

Illustrator
Christy Verna

Copywriter
Patrick Smith

Printer
Merit Press

The two-color label uses recycled stock and is printed with soy inks. The finished product is a heart-warming gift packaged with sensitivity and respect for the environment.

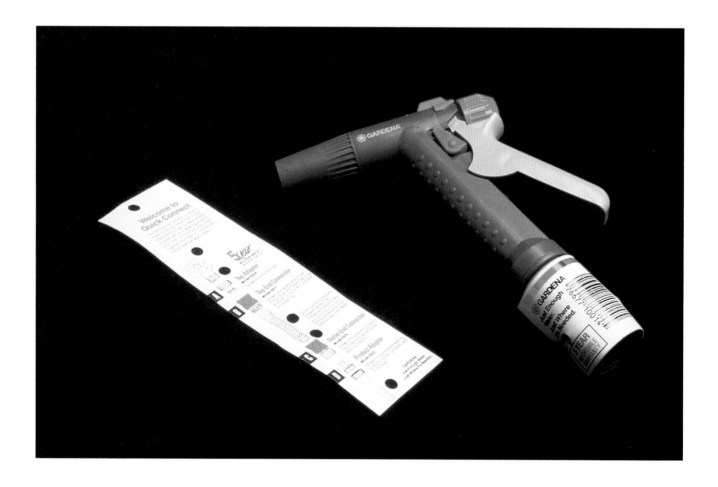

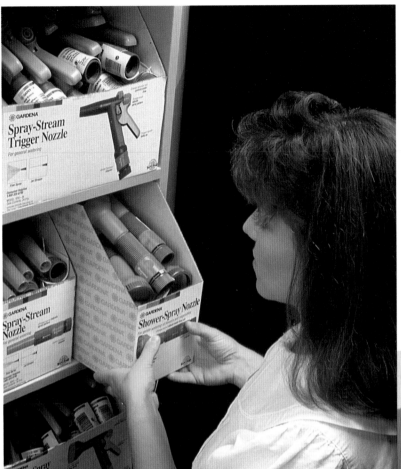

**Gardena UN-Packaging
and Merchandising**

Design Firm
Fitch Inc.

Art Director
Marla Aberegg

Designer
**Roger Pinnick,
Jacquie Richmond**

Photographer
Mark Steele, Fitch

Client
Gardena, division of Gale Group

Fitch created a more environmentally responsible system that "bulk-merchandises" sprinkler products and connectors to eliminate secondary packaging. Products are held in bins that organize them for easy inventory control and re-stocking.

Ann Taylor

Design Firm	Photographer
Cato Gobé & Associates	**J.R. Durand**
Creative Director	Client
Marc Gobé	**Ann Taylor**
Art Director	Copywriter
Peter Levine	**Cato Gobé & Associates**
Designer	Printer
Peter Levine	**Wright Packaging**

The Ann Taylor packaging communicates an image that is natural, honest, and personal. Made from recycled and recyclable materials, the paper's natural color and texture convey ease and authenticity. Details like new box shapes, navy grosgrain ribbon, and the photograph of a smiling Ann Taylor woman, add character and personality to the total concept.

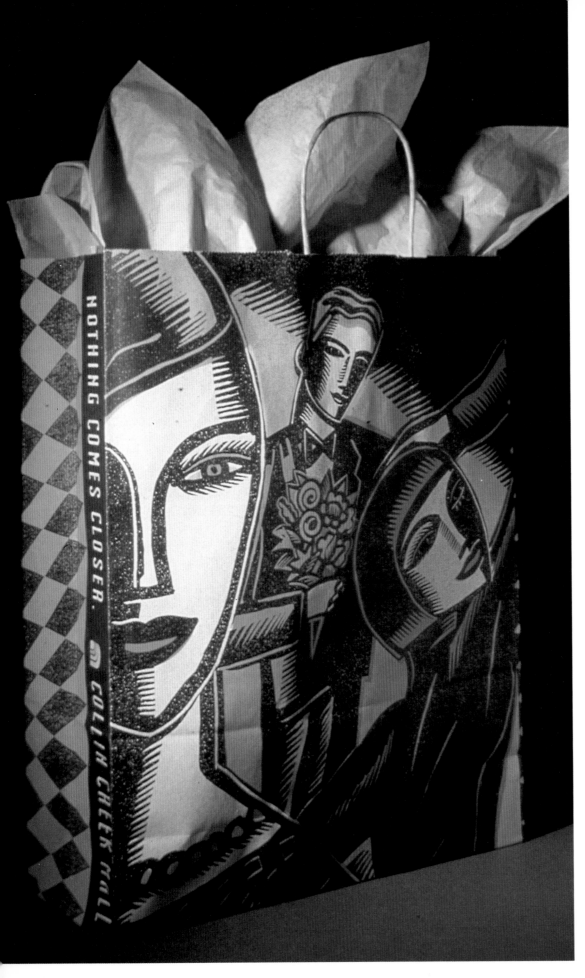

Collin Creek Shopping Bag

Design Firm
Sibley/Peteet Design, Inc.

Art Director
Rex Peteet

Designer
Rex Peteet, Julia Albanesi

Illustrator
Anthony Russo

Client
Colin Creek Mall

The bag is constructed of 100% recycled paper.

Autumn Harp
Identity/Packaging

Design Firm
Jager Di Paola Kemp Design

Art Director
Michael Jager/
Giovanna Jager

Designer
Giovanna Jager

Illustrator
Tom Patrick

Client
Autumn Harp

This minimal display structure
is printed in two colors and
made with 100% recycled
packaging board.

Snowboard Wax POP

Design Firm
Jager Di Paola Kemp Design

Art Director
Michael Jager, David Covell

Designer
Adam Levite

Client
XXX Snowboard Wax

This point of purchase display
uses recyclable corrugated
cardboard and allows for
minimal product packaging.

**Gilbert Paper Sales/
Promotion Portfolio**

Design Firm
Grafik Communications Ltd.

Design Team
**Melanie Bass, Gregg Glaviano,
Judy F. Kirpich**

Photographer
Claude Vasquez

Illustrator
Betsy Shields

Client
Gilbert Paper

Copywriter
Jake Pollard

Printer
VA Lithograph

Production/Printing
**Soy-based inks, offset
with die-cut folder**

**The entire kit was printed with
soy-based inks. Recyclable
E-Flute, plain wood sticks, and
twine were used for the box.**

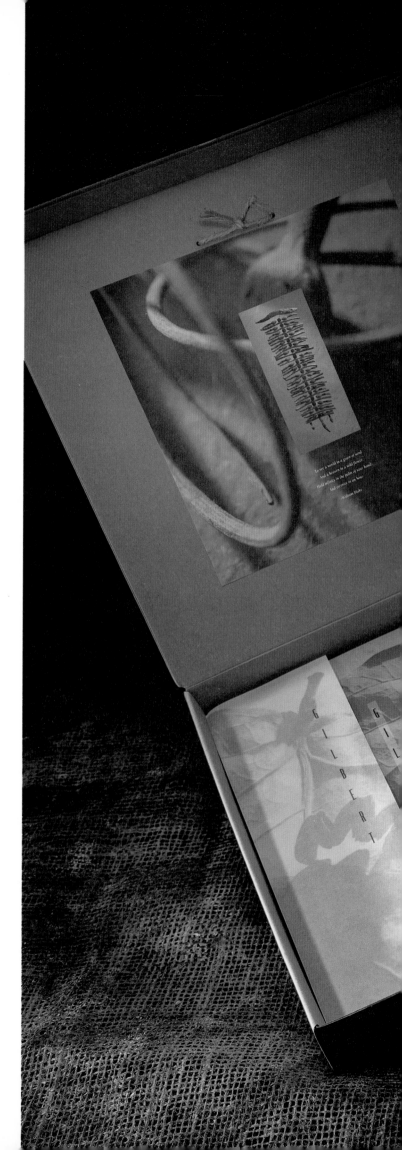

Abercrombie & Fitch
(This spread and overleaf)

Design Firm
Cato Gobé & Associates

Creative Director
Marc Gobé

Art Director
Bill Hovard

Designer
Alexandra Min, Thomas Davidson, Marion Cledat, Claudia Brandenberg

Photographer
Robert Whitman

Illustrator
Thomas Davidson

Client
Abercrombie & Fitch

Copywriter
Cato Gobé & Associates

Printer
Interstate

Production/Printing
Offset, recycled paper

Inspired by the Adirondacks, the most recent line of packaging for Abercrombie & Fitch uses burlap sacks, heavy cardboard boxes, and metal canisters to package the store's utilitarian clothing and accessories. All of the materials are either readily recyclable, or recycled.

Tabaco Ornelas

Design Firm
Luis Fitch Diseño

Art Director/Designer/Illustrator
Luis Fitch

Photographer
Paul Brown

Client
Tabaco Ornelas, S.A.

The actual cigar box is made from non-endangered species of trees found in the jungles of Chiapas, Mexico. The package label is printed in Mexico on recycled paper.

Mission Store

Design Firm
Weber Design Partners, Inc.

Art Director
Christina Weber

Designer
Marty Gregg

Client
Perkins Shear Stores

Copywriter
Mary Gregg

Production/Printing
Foil stamp, Offset

All paper is 100% recycled to make the packaging fit the image of the store.

Mezcal Avila

Design Firm
Luis Fitch Diseño

Art Director/Designer/Illustrator
Luis Fitch

Photographer
Mark Stele

Client
Mexcal Avila Oaxaca

Copywriter
Juan Soldado

Printer
Impresora Oaxaca

Package design intended to reflect a unique product from Mexico. Whenever possible, natural recyclable materials were utilized. All bottles are hand wrapped with Maguay fibers by local artisans. The label is printed on recycled paper in one color with soy-based ink.

Earth Preserv

Design Firm
Peterson & Company

Art Director
Jan Wilson

Designer/Illustrator
Jan Wilson/Bryan L. Peterson

Client
Peterson & Company

Printer
Advanced Monobloc

Earth Preserv bath and skin products are totally recyclable. The aluminum can contains no plastic parts and the ingredients are all naturally derived. The soaps are wrapped in foil for recycling purposes. Aluminum is one of the most recyclable of materials and is always in demand.

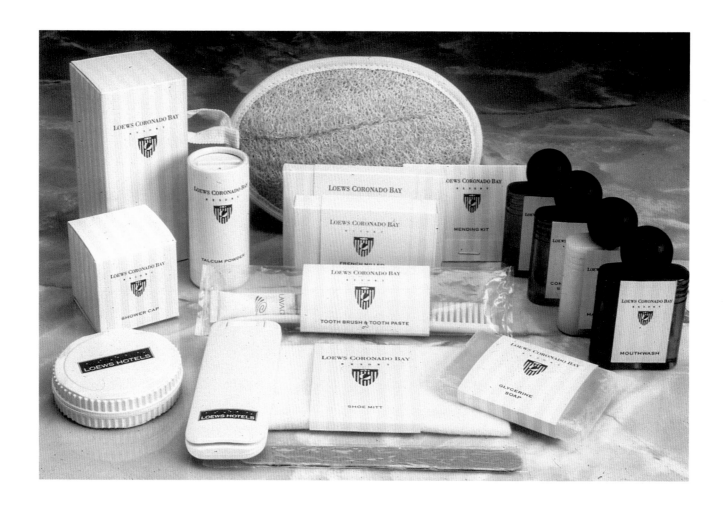

**Loews Hotels
Personal Amenities**

Design Firm
Lebowitz/Gould/Design, Inc.

Art Director
Sue Gould, Susan Chait

Designer
Susan Chait

Client
Loews Hotels

**Recyclable plastics were used
for all packaging. All labels and
boxes have light ink coverage
on recycled stock.**

Wood Collection Line

Design Firm
**Maurizio di Robilant
& Associates**

Art Director
Maurizio di Robilant

Designer
**Maurizio di Robilant/
Lucia Jommarsa**

Client
Koh-I-Noor SpA–Italia

The wood collection line has
been entirely produced using
recyclable materials. All of the
packaging requires only one
glue point, and illustrations
have been employed to avoid
the use of plastics and acetates.

Sunrise Packaging

Design Firm
Mires Design, Inc.

Art Director/Designer
Scott Mires

Illustrator
Tracy Sabin

Client
Sunrise Publications, Ltd.

Copywriter
Kelly Smothermon

Printed on recycled paper.

Deleo Color Blend Packaging

Design Firm
Mires Design, Inc.

Art Director/Designer
José Serrano

Illustrator
Nancy Stahl

Client
Deleo Clay Tile Company

Copywriter
Kelly Smothermon

Printer
Rush Press

This company uses natural
ingredients in all of its products
and likes to extend this image
by using recycled materials in
their packaging.

Promotional Oil

Design Firm
Burkur Design Group

Art Director
Patricia Burkur

Designer
Patricia Burkur/Nin D Useja

Photographer
Gordon Meyer

Recycled packing material was used to protect the bottled oil. The label was printed on an Iris dye sublimation printer on recycled paper. Recipients of the self-promotional piece recycle the wood boxes as storage crates.

INDIAN

POSTERS

Marshall McLuhan said "The medium is the message," and posters with an environmental twist get the message across well. Some of the pieces in this section have a purely environmental message—some have environmental elements and extend a totally different message. In either case, posters are a great way to promote kindness to the environment.

Sonic Youth Poster

Design Firm
Geffen Records

Art Director/Designer/Illustrator
Kevin Reagan

The poster uses recycled butcher paper with minimal prepress work to reduce the amount of chemicals used in production.

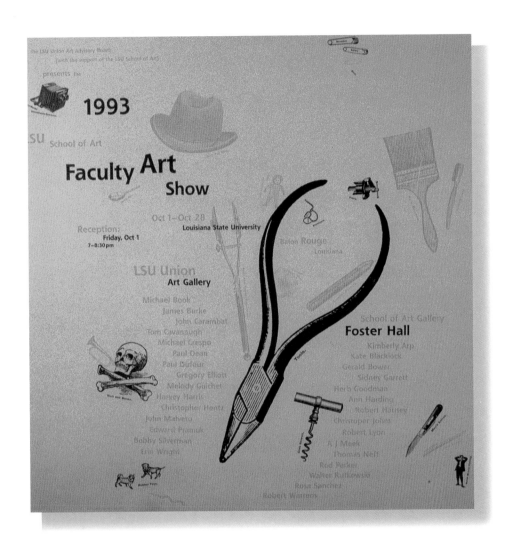

Faculty Art Show

Design Firm
Paper Shrine

Art Director
Paul Dean

Designer
Paul Dean

Client
Louisiana State University

Copywriter
Judy Stahl

Printer
Graphic Services, Inc.

Production/Printing
2-color Offset, including fluorescent orange.

This poster was printed on 100% recycled paper; the playful use of images from an early Sears Roebuck catalog reinforces the notion of "recycling." The poster also folds up and serves as its own mailer, thereby eliminating the need for additional packaging.

AIGA Business of Graphic Design Seminar Poster

Design Firm
Joseph Rattan Design

Art Director/Copy
Joseph Rattan

Designer
Greg Morgan

Illustrator
Linda Helton

Client
AIGA, Texas

Printer
Heritage Press

Printed on 100% recycled Simpson Equinox

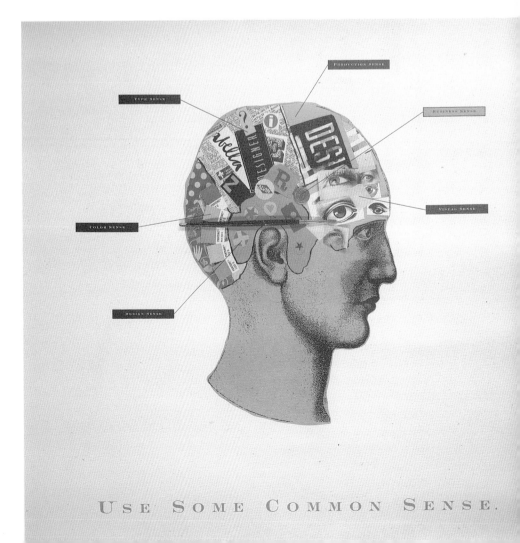

USE SOME COMMON SENSE.

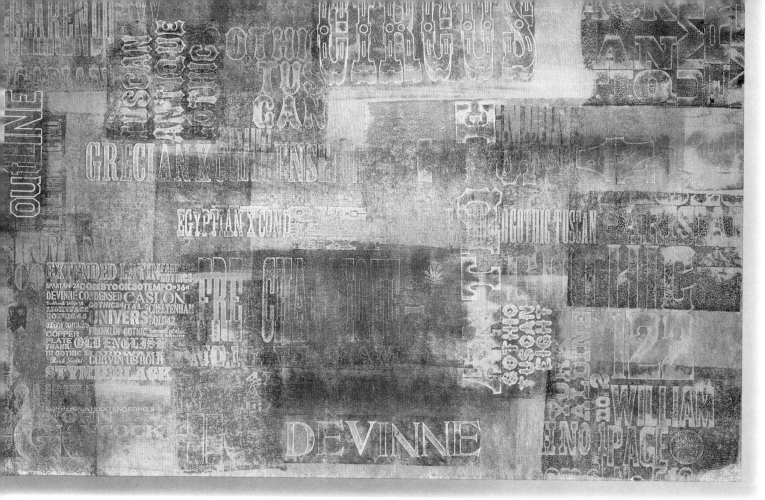

Devinne

Design Firm
Segura, Inc.

Art Director/Designer
**Carlos Segura and
Hatch Show Print**

Client
AGFA

Printer
Hatch Show Print

Hatch Show Print uses "plates" carved from wooden blocks and minimal chemistry in its printing process.

Pricing Game Poster

Design Firm
The Leonhardt Group

Art Director
Dennis Clouse

Designers
Dennis Clouse, Traci Daberko, Charlyne Fabi, Kaitlin Snyder, Jeff Welsh

Client
Graphic Artist Guild, Seattle

Copy
Karen Wilson

Printer
The Copy Company

This poster is printed on used chipboard that was going to be discarded. The board's texture enhances the graphics and gives the poster a game board quality.

HKIPP Awards Exhibition

Design Firm
**Kan Tài-keung Design &
Associates, Ltd.**

Art Director
Freeman Lau Siu Hong

Designer
**Freeman Lau Siu Hong/
Eric Cheung**

Photographer
C. K. Wong

Client
**Hong Kong Institute of
Professional Photographers Ltd.**

Printer
Hoi Kwong Printing Co. Ltd.

This poster is an appraisal
of excellent work done by
photographers participating
in an exhibition. It is printed
on recycled paper.

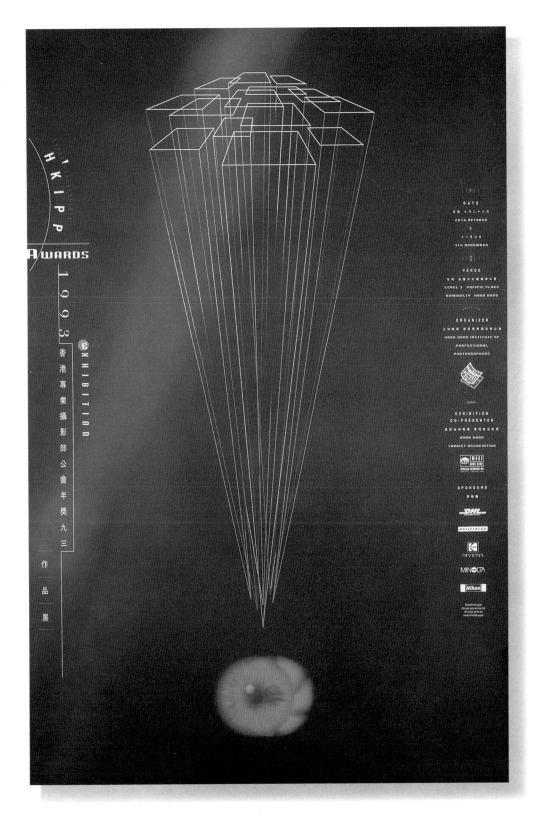

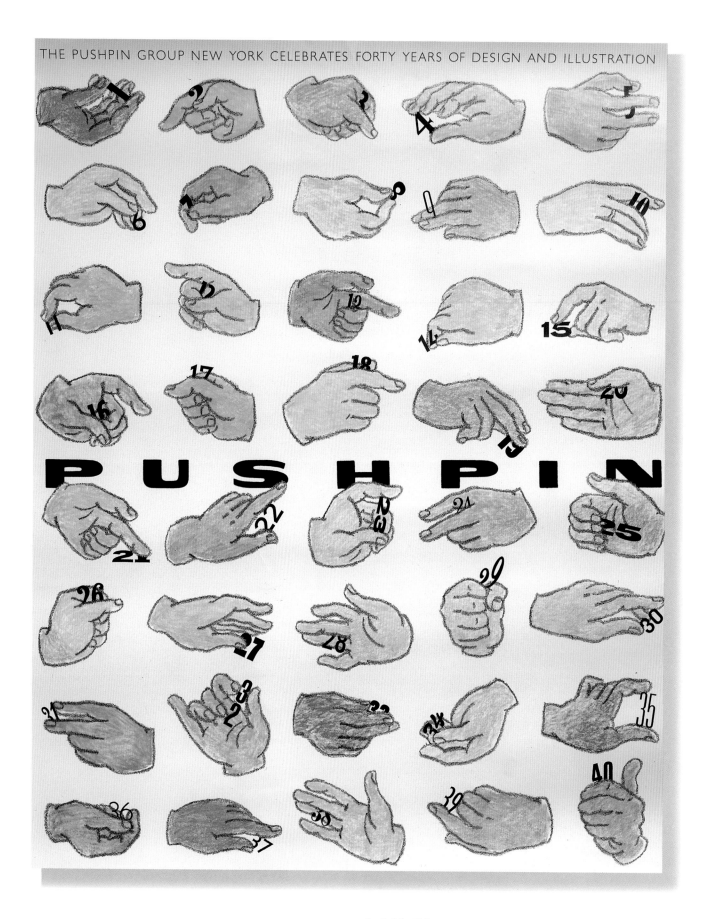

Pushpin's 40th
Anniversary poster

Design Firm
The Pushpin Group

Art Director/Designer/Illustrator
Seymour Chwast

A limited run of posters were
printed on recycled paper.

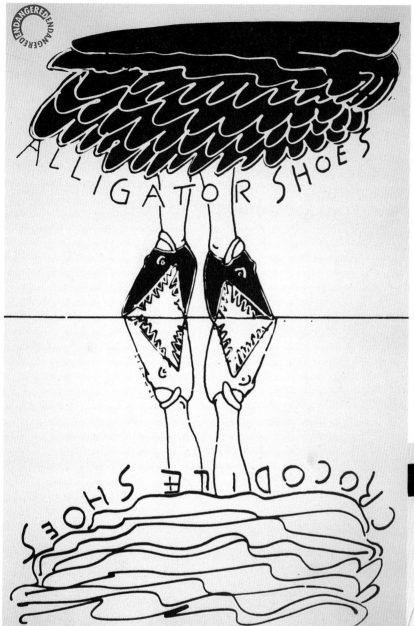

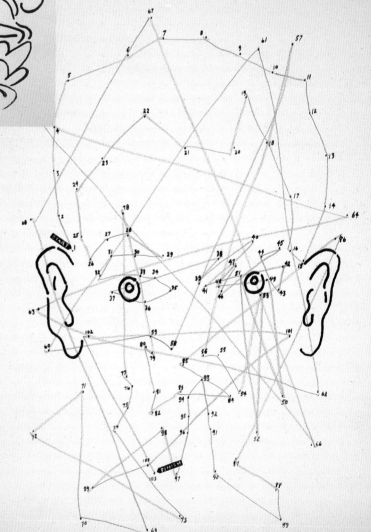

Endangered
(this spread and overleaf)

Design Firm
Sommese Design

Art Director
Lanny Sommese

Designer
Lanny Sommese

Illustrator
Lanny Sommese

Client
**Penn State Institute for Arts
and Humanistic Studies**

Printer
Jim Lilly

Production/Printing
Silkscreen

**Subject matter relates all
the posters in this series,
which were all printed on
recycled paper.**

CHEETAH

PANTHER

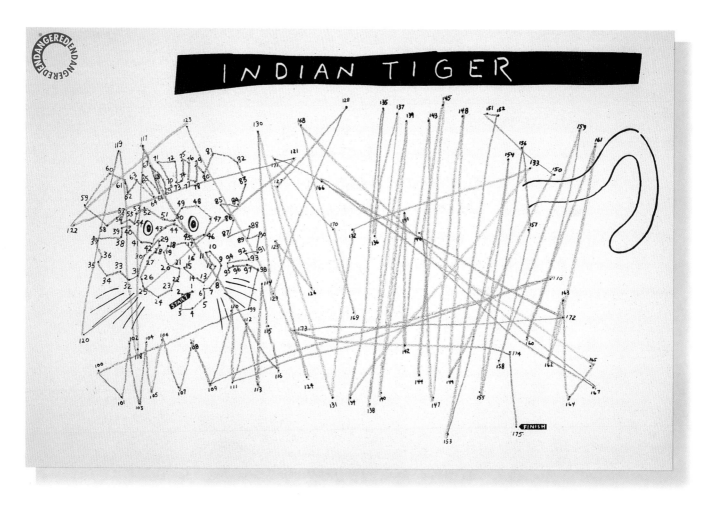

INDIAN TIGER

Join Up
(previous page)

Design Firm
Michael Schwab Design

Designer
Michael Schwab

Illustrator
Michael Schwab

Client
Oklahoma State University

Printer
Rob Murray & Co.

Production/Printing
One-color screen printing on recycled paper

Red Sky Films

Design Firm
Michael Schwab Design

Art Director
Steve Zeifman

Designer
Michael Schwab

Illustrator
Michael Schwab

Client
Red Sky Films

Printer
Rob Murray & Co.

Production/Printing
One-color screen printing on recycled paper

Save me, please. I'm here.

Save Me, Please. I'm Here.

Design Firm
Nippon Design Center, Inc.

Art Director
Kazumasa Nagai

Designer
Kazumasa Nagai

Client
Self-Promotion

Production/Printing
Silkscreen

These posters, silkscreened on recycled paper address an ecological issue more through their message than their production. The striking images are effective in projecting their ecological image to wide audiences. The artists says, "The reason I depict living creatures in my drawings is my philosophy that this earth belongs not only to humans, but any living thing.

Bay to Bay

Design Firm
Mires Design, Inc.

Art Director/Designer
Jose Serrano

Illustrator
Gerald Bustamante

Client
Peninsula Family YMCA

Printer
Bordeaux Printers

The illustrator recycled used cardboard and then painted the illustration on it, producing a great effect.

Bay to Bay Poster

Design Firm
Mires Design, Inc.

Art Director/Designer
Jose Serrano

Illustrator
Tracy Sabin

Client
Peninsula Family YMCA

Printer
Gordon Silkscreener

The poster was screen printed on Simpson Quest, a recycled paper containing 100% post-consumer waste.

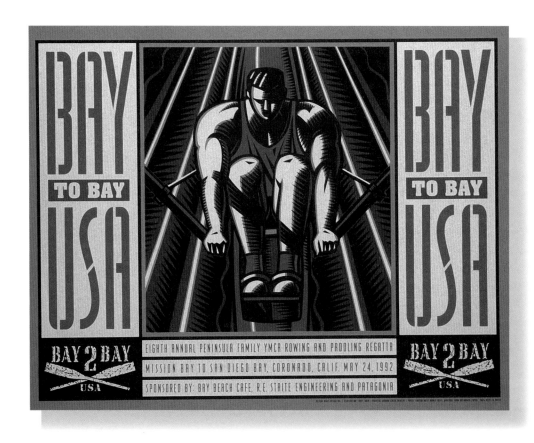

Jazz–"Hot as Hell"

Design Firm
Sommese Design

Art Director
Lanny Sommese

Designer
Lanny Sommese

Illustrator
Lanny Sommese

Client
Penn State Jazz Club

Printer
Penn State Design Practicum

The poster was printed on recycled paper using water-based silk screen techniques.

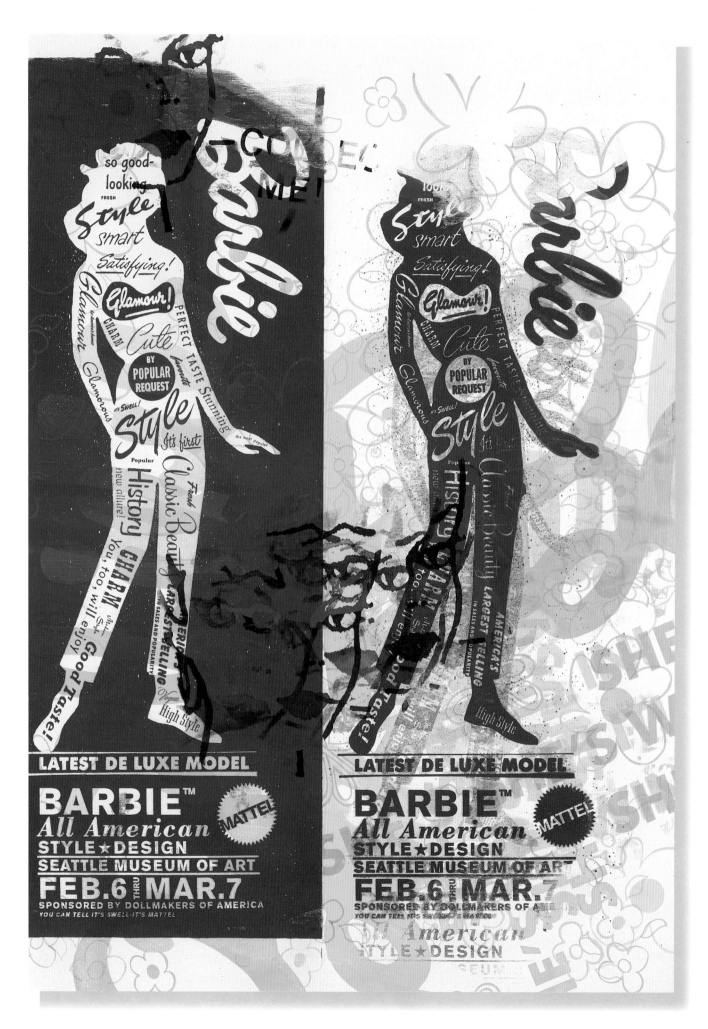

Personal Work

Design Firm
Modern Dog

Art Directors/Designers/
Illustrators/Copywriters
**Robynne Raye,
Michael Strassburger,
and Vittorio Costarella**

Client
Modern Dog

Printer
Joe Barella

Production/Printing
Screen printing

A screen printing friend of the
designer, Joe Barella, had a lot
of left-over inks and scrap
paper, so he said, "Hey Joe,
can we do something fun with
all my leftover junk?"

We Do Our Art

Design Firm
Planet Design Company

Art Director
Kevin Wade, Dana Lytle

Designer
Kevin Wade, Dana Lytle

Client
**Art Directors
Association of Iowa**

These silk-screened posters are printed on French Dur-O-Tone recycled paper. All art was created with conventional production techniques.

**Louisiana Coalition
for Tax Justice**

Design Firm
Planet Design Company

Art Director
Kevin Wade, Dana Lytle

Designer
Kevin Wade, Erik Johnson

Illustrator
Erik Johnson

Client
**Louisiana Coalition
for Tax Justice**

Copy
Zack Nauth

This poster was printed in one color on recycled stock.

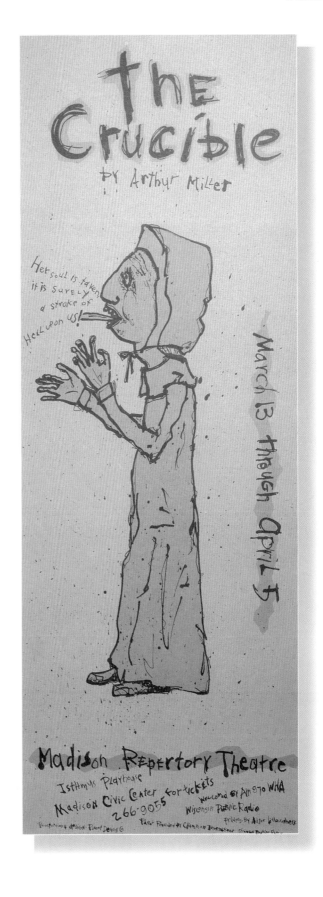

The Crucible Posters

Design Firm
Planet Design Company

Designer
Kevin Wade

Client
Madison Repertory Theatre

Art Director
Kevin Wade, Dana Lytle

Illustrator
Kevin Wade

Printer
Adtec Lithographics

The posters are printed on remnant Simpson Evergreen stock with promotional images on the front and back.

The Green Island

Design Firm
Leslie Chan Design Co., Ltd.

Art Director
Leslie Chan Wing Kei

Designer
Leslie Chan Wing Kei

Client
**Taiwan Image Poster
Design Association**

This series of posters promotes environmentally sound principles through striking artwork.

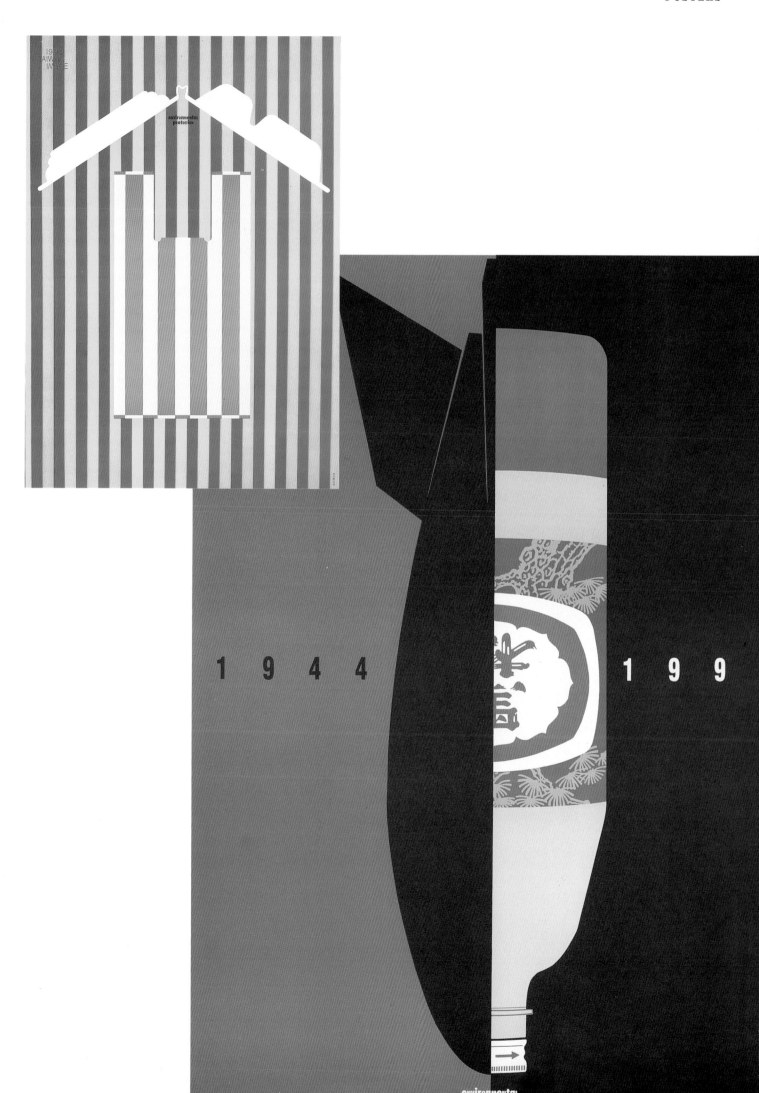

Yohji Yamamoto

Design Firm
Petrick Design

Art Director
Robert Petrick

Designer
Laura Ress

Photographer
Robert Petrick

Client
June Blaker

Copy
Wim Wenders

Printer
Rohner Printing Company

Posters were cut into 16
postcards that were each mailed
as announcements or handed
out as flyers. All promotional
materials for this film/fashion
show were created with one
printing job.

104

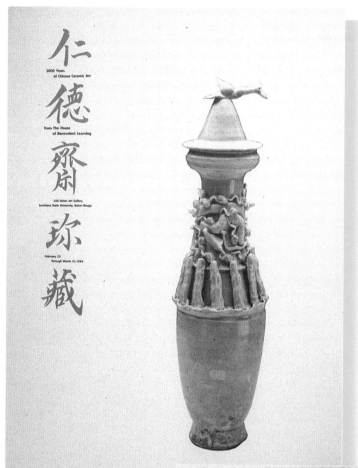

3,000 Years of Chinese Ceramic Art

Design Firm
Paper Shrine

Art Director/Designer
Paul Dean

Client
Louisiana State University

Copy
Rikki Scollard

Printer
Graphic Services, Inc.

This poster was printed on 100% recycled paper with visible pulp and texture to suggest ancient Chinese paper. It also serves as a reminder of the Chinese invention of the paper-making process, and encourages the awareness of the organic sources of all paper.

**Central Pennsylvania
Festival of the Arts**
(facing page)

Design Firm
Sommese Design

Art Director/Designer/Illustrator
Lanny Sommese

Client
**Central Pennsylvania
Festival of the Arts**

Copy
Cathy Talcott

**This poster is printed Offset
on recycled paper.**

Why? No!

Design Firm
Sommese Design

Art Director/Designer/Illustrator
Lanny Sommese

These limited run posters were
silk-screened on recycled paper
to increase awareness of the
ecological impact of war.

Adirondack chair

véritable institution américaine
depuis plus de 150 ans,
la chaise Adirondack invite à
s'y étendre par temps chaud
pour siroter un thé glacé.

robe 495F

BROCHURES

Brochures—organizations large and small crank them out faster than people can throw them away. This section features both innovative and conventional ideas that work toward protecting the environment while still getting the client's message out on a printed piece.

**Wilderness Products Inc.
Catalog**

Design Firm
Richardson or Richardson

Art Director
Forrest Richardson

Designer
Neill Fox

Photographer
Keith Alstin

Client
**Wilderness
Products, Inc.**

Copywriter
**Forrest Richardson,
Neill Fox**

Printer
Web Crafters

**The cover of this catalog is
recycled Kraft, inside pages
are printed on newsprint,
one of the original recycled
printing papers. Photographs
of the items used to construct
the products (zipper pulls, etc.)
were done on a photocopier,
eliminating chemicals needed
to develop film.**

AIGA Conference Book

Design Firm
Little & Company

Art Director
Paul Wharton

Designer
Ellen Huber

Illustrator
J. Otto Siebold

Client
Cross Pointe Paper Corporation

Printer
Dan Wallace

The objective of this promotion was threefold: to demonstrate the printability of Cross Pointe's recycled papers; to encourage designers to specify Cross Pointe recycled papers; and to be useful to designers. The client wanted to create something that had a purpose beyond promoting a product and could be kept, used, and re-used.

ECODEA (Environmental Graphic Design Consultancy)

Design Firm
Richardson or Richardson

Art Director
Forrest and Valerie Richardson

Designer
Debi Young Mees

Illustrator
Richardson or Richardson staff

Client
ECODEA

Copy
Forrest Richardson

Printer
McGrew Printing

This brochure was printed with handset metal type, eliminating the need for films, plates or chemicals. It was constructed with recycled chipboard, printed with water-based ink, and bound with a screwset (avoiding harmful glues and plastics).

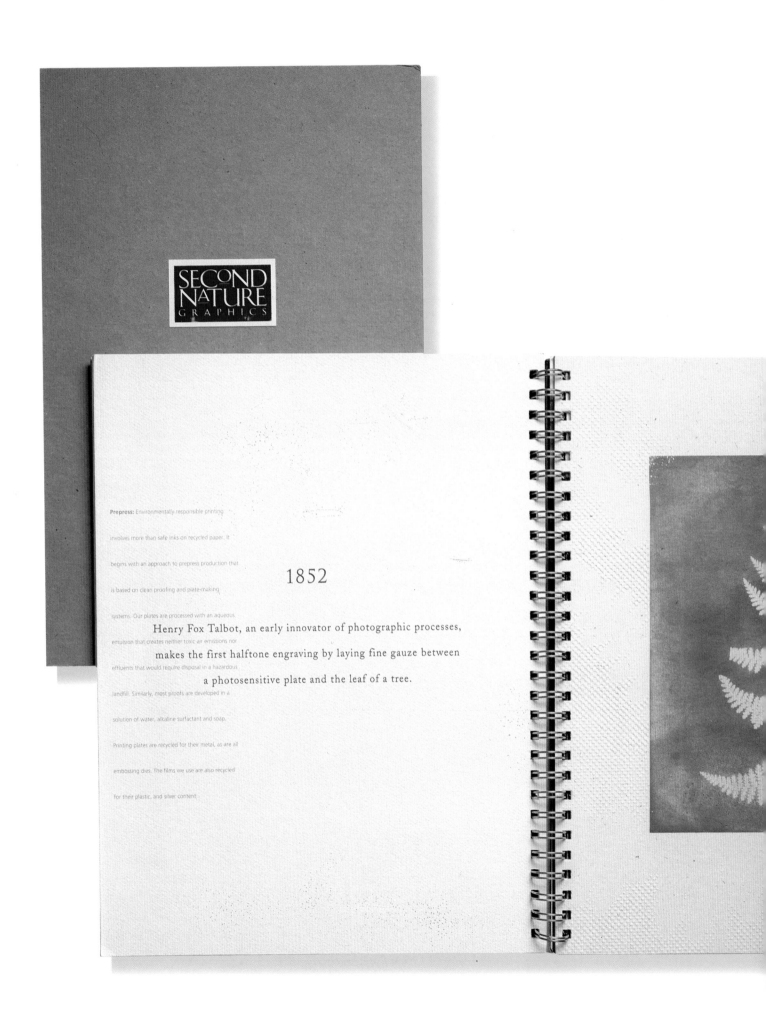

Prepress: Environmentally-responsible printing

involves more than safe inks on recycled paper. It

begins with an approach to prepress production that

is based on clean proofing and plate-making

systems. Our plates are processed with an aqueous

emulsion that creates neither toxic air emissions nor

effluents that would require disposal in a hazardous

landfill. Similarly, most proofs are developed in a

solution of water, alkaline surfactant and soap.

Printing plates are recycled for their metal, as are all

embossing dies. The films we use are also recycled

for their plastic, and silver content.

1852

Henry Fox Talbot, an early innovator of photographic processes,

makes the first halftone engraving by laying fine gauze between

a photosensitive plate and the leaf of a tree.

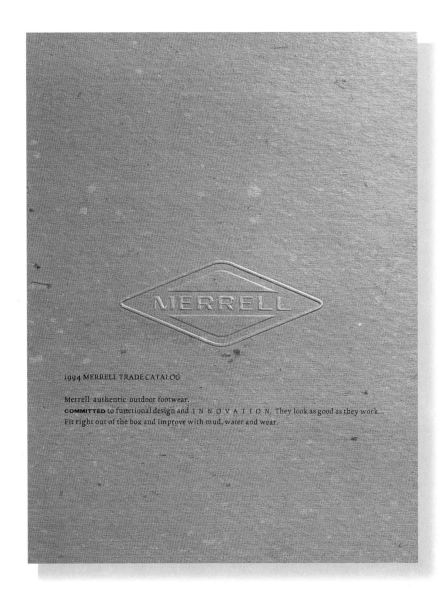

Second Nature Graphics

Design Firm
**Eric Baker Design
Associates, Inc.**

Art Director
Eric Baker

Designer
Eric Baker, Patrick Seymour

Client
Second Nature Graphics, Inc.

Copywriter
David Koenigsberg

Printer
Second Nature Graphics

This pages of this brochure booklet were printed on recycled paper. The cover is plain Kraft without lamination or coating.

Merrell Trade Catalog

Design Firm
Jager Di Paola Kemp Design

Art Director
Michael Jager, Steve Farrar

Designer
Steve Farrar, Holly Boardman, Kirk James

Photographer
Scott Ryder

Client
Merrell

Printer
O'Keefe Printing

Merrell Trade's catalog cover is 100% recycled French packing carton, which is made of large chunks of post-consumer waste which has not been de-inked.

Capp Street Project
Membership Brochure

Design Firm
Morla Design

Art Director
Jennifer Morla

Designer
Jennifer Morla, Sharrie Brooks

Client
Capp Street Project

Printer
Venture Graphics

This brochure and accompanying materials are printed on Simpson Quest, a recycled stock containing 100% post-consumer waste that has not been de-inked.

SEGD What Works

Design Firm
Stoltze Design

Art Director
Clifford Stoltze

Designer
**Clifford Stoltze, Peter Farrell,
Rebecca Fagan**

Photographer
**Allan Shortall, Carol Naughton,
Barbara Karant, R. Greg
Hursley, Randolph Janu**

Client
**Society for Environmental
Graphic Design**

Printer
Arlington Litho

Printed on Fox River Confetti,
a 100% recycled paper
containing at least 50%
post-consumer waste.

**San Francisco
International Airport
Annual Report**

Design Firm
Morla Design

Art Director
Jennifer Morla

Designer
Jennifer Morla, Craig Baily

Photographer
Holly Stewart Photography

Client
**San Francisco Airport
Commission**

Copywriter
Airport Staff

Printer
Fong & Fong

Production/Printing
Simpson Gainsborough paper

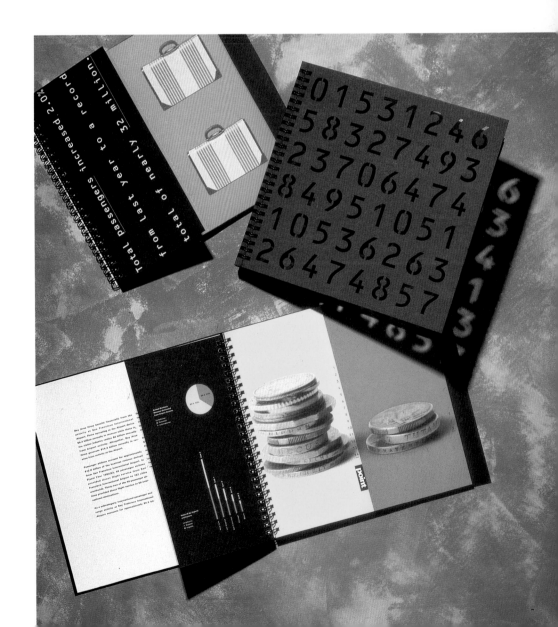

American Heart Association of Metro Chicago Annual Report

Design Firm
Samata Associates

Art Director
Pat & Greg Samata

Designer
Pat & Greg Samata, Dan Kraemer

Photographer
Marc Norberg

Client
American Heart Association of Metro Chicago

Copywriter
Liz Horan

Printer
Columbia Graphics Corporation

Production/Printing
4-color process, PMS, spot varnish

Stitching was used for binding, eliminating the need for glue. The book is printed entirely on 100% recycled French Butcher paper.

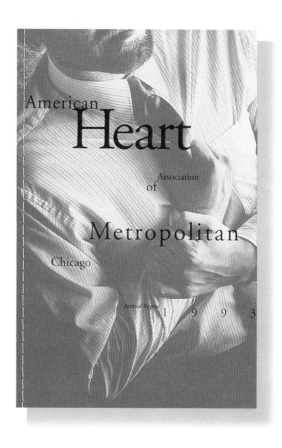

The American Heart Association of Metropolitan Chicago is in the business of saving lives.

This process begins with research and results in programs delivered at the community level. • Research is the starting point. Our current knowledge about the causes, treatment and

prevention of heart disease and stroke comes from years of biomedical research. Our own

Dear Friends

commitment to research is strong: in 1992-93, we allocated close to $1 million in research awards, the largest amount in our history. • In turn, discoveries made in the laboratory inform and shape all AHA programs. With heart disease prevention and early intervention

as our primary commitments, we reached 432,750 people with programs in schools, at work and in the community. • These research and prevention efforts are paying off. Death rates

from heart disease are declining significantly. But while we have made great progress,

cardiovascular diseases remain our nation's — and the Chicago area's — number one cause

of death. Our cause is urgent and requires our continued efforts to raise the dollars needed to fund research and programs throughout the Chicago area. • This report celebrates the partnership between research and program as well as the accomplishments of the past year.

1992-93 was a year of change. Under new leadership, AHA-MC moved its central office

and undertook a staff restructuring, resulting in substantial long-term savings. And we launched an ambitious community organization effort with the goal of developing 20

branches in metropolitan Chicago by 1996. • Thanks to the dedication of volunteers, contributors and staff, the American Heart Association of Metropolitan Chicago is ready

to meet the challenges ahead. Our success will be measured by the lives we change and

the lives we save. ♥

Henry L. Kohn, Chairman (right) • Lawrence L. Michaelis, M.D., President (bottom) Almarie Wagner, Executive Director (top)

**Lifeco Travel Services/
American Express Brochure**

Design Firm
Peat Jariya Design

Art Director/Designer
Peat Jariya

Photographer
Steve Chen

Client
**Lifeco/American Express
Travel Services**

Printer
Boehm

The brochure is printed in six
colors on recycled paper.

Cigna Bicentennial

Design Firm
**Thom & Dave
Marketing Design, Inc.**

Art Director
Thom Holden, Dave Bell

Designer
Dave Bell

Photographer
Seymour Mednick

Illustrator
**Thom Holden, Seymour
Mednick, Dave Bell**

Client
Cigna Corporation

Copywriter
Warren Levy, Cigna

Printer
Pearl Pressman Liberty

This brochure is printed offset
and embossed on recycled coat-
ed and uncoated stocks.

Passy Plaza
Opening Booklet/Paris

Design Firm
Gap Advertising

Creative Director
Maggie Gross

Designer
Siras Greiner

Photographer
Patrick Demarchelier

Illustrator
Alexis MacDonald

Client
Gap International

Copywriter
Anne Buhl

Print Production
Manager Norine Araiza

Printer
Mastercraft Press

Gap Advertising uses paper with 50% recycled content with at least 10% post-consumer waste. The company specifies soy-based inks whenever possible, and does not use metallic inks.

The Agfatype Idea Catalogue

Design Firm
Segura, Inc.

Art Director/Designer
Carlos Segura

Illustrator
Stephen Farrel

Client
AGFA

This promotional brochure
for AGFA's type business is
printed 4-color web on
newsprint, a recycled and
recyclable stock—a great
alternative to conventional
premium printing papers.
The cover is printed in Hatch
Show print with wood type.

The VH-1 Awards

Design Firm
Werner Design Werks Inc.

Art Director
Sharon Werner

Designers/Illustrators
**Sharon Werner,
Amy Quinlivan**

Photographer
**Lizzie Himmel, Paul Irmiter,
Photonica, Shawn Smith**

Client
VH-1 Networks

Printer
Heartland Graphics

The client needed a small quantity of this piece, so the job was planned so that all the pages fit on one press form. The book was attached to a pocket so that updates could be added. The pockets were manufactured from existing envelopes (two pockets were made from each envelope.) This well thought-out publication is environmentally friendly because it uses minimal materials while maintaining a high visual impact.

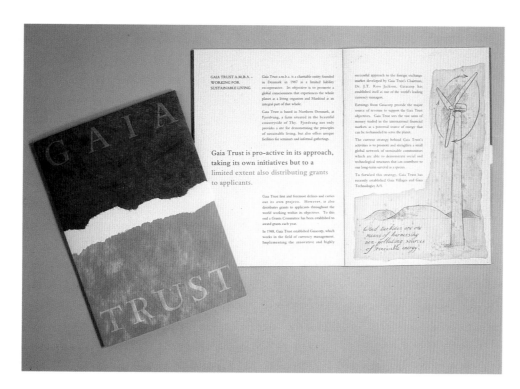

Gaia Trust Brochure

Design Firm
Design House Consultants

Art Director
Chris Lower

Designer
Katie Arup

Illustrator
Alan Magowen

Client
Gaiacorp

Printer
Tradewinds

Gaia Trust is a charitable
organization created to promote
global consciousness and the
environment. The brochure
was printed on recycled
paper in three colors.

Converse Trade Catalog
(bottom)

Design Firm
Jager Di Paola Kemp Design

Art Director
Michael Jager, Steve Farrar

Designer
Steve Farrar

Photographer
**Aaron Warkoy, Peter Rice,
Michael Jager**

Client
Converse

Printer
W. E. Andrews

This promotional brochure for
Converse uses 100% recycled
French Speckletone for the
cover and single-color printing
throughout.

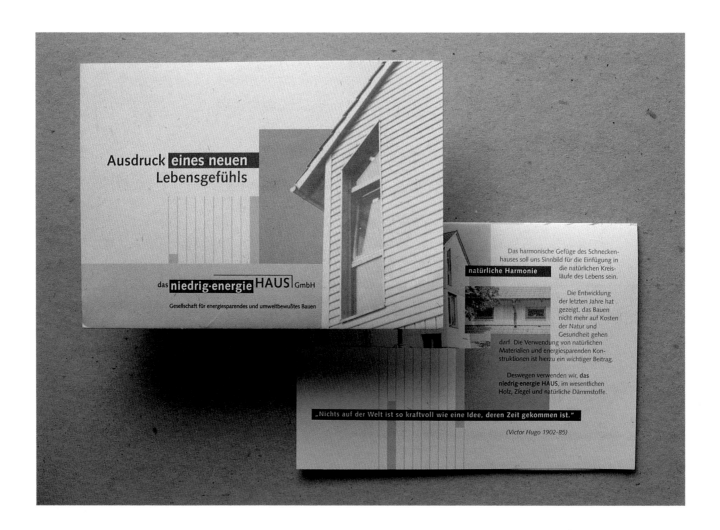

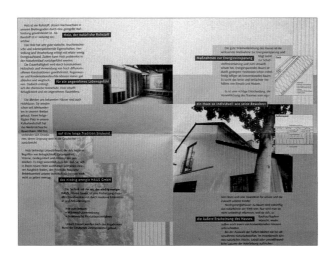

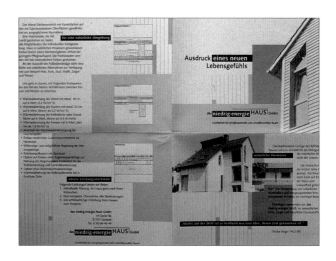

Lebensgeful-Art of Living

Design Firm
CAW

Art Director/Designer
Carsten-Andres Werner

Client
**das niedrig · energie
HAUS GmbH**

The das niedrig · energie HAUS GmbH is a bureau of two architects who build houses made of natural and recycled materials. The use of these materials helps to cut down on costs and waste of natural resources. The brochure uses recycled paper containing 100% post-consumer waste paper.

Design Factory Celebrate 10

Design Firm
Design Factory

Photographer
Walter Pfeiffer

Copy
Mel Clark

Printer
Euroscreen

The entire brochure was printed on recycled paper.

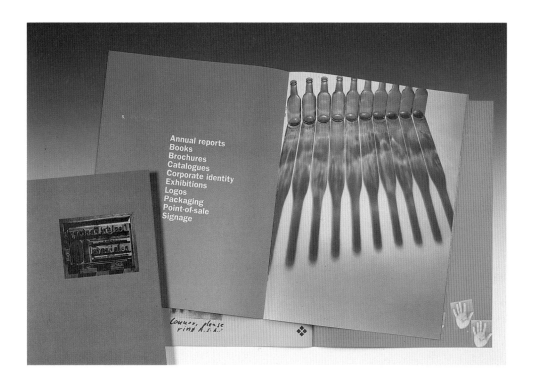

**Celeste Cuomo:
The Environment**

Design Firm
Mires Design

Art Director/Designer
Walter Pfeiffer

Client
Celeste Cuomo

Copy
Robert Goldstein

Printed on recycled paper, this promotional brochure showcases illustrators and gives suggestions on how to help preserve the environment.

WINE N LIST

MISCELLANEOUS

Annual Reports, Invitations, Greeting Cards, and more.

1994

VH-1 HONORS

This Book Belongs to:

_____

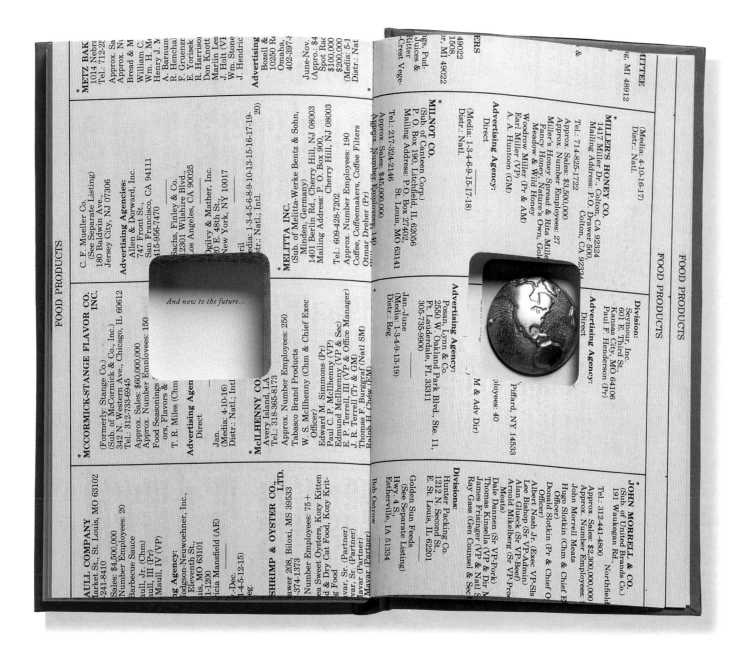

And now to the future...

VH-1 Honors

Design Firm
Werner Design Werks

Art Director
Cheri Dorr, Sharon Werner

Designer
Sharon Werner

Client
VH-1 Network

Copy
Dan Hedges

Printer
Diversified Graphics; Bindery, Midwest Additions

Production/Printing
Offset, Foil Stamping

The VH-1 Honors event awards a group of musicians who have contributed greatly to a charity or organization of their choice. The program book works as a biography of the chosen artists, and is a commemorative piece for the first annual event. The surprise comes in the middle of the book which opens to a small jewel-like world protected within the confines of a diecut opening, much like the tradition of hiding valuables inside thick books for safe keeping. The diecut portion of the book is made up of "retired" books from the library. The books are out-of-date unsalvagable text books, almanacs, or books with badly destroyed covers. Approximately 4,000 old books were used to make 10,000 new books. VH-1 gave the books new life and made a donation to the Friends of the Minneapolis Library to be used for new books as well as a donation to the Literacy Volunteers of America.

FABULA
INSTITUTE
of ANCIENT
STUDIES

Dr. O. Cyrus, Ph.D., D.D.
Rector
Centre for Classical Research
Grove of Diana Boulevard
Adnaron

St. John Ave.
notoha
JN8 7HH

FABULA

Firebir

F E N I X

INTRODUCTION

The most auspicious day of my life start-
ed inauspiciously indeed. I was shiver-
ing in my tent (it can get surprisingly
cold on the plateau between Pyramis and
Thisbe) waiting for the tea that would bring
some warmth to my limbs, when I heard
Vassiliou shouting from down the slope. "Boss,
boss," he cried. He had been my lead digger for
more than ten years, and so formality had

naturally vanished between us. I did think it
unfortunate, however, that so much of his spare
time seemed to be taken up watching re-runs of
Fantasy Island.

"Boss, boss," I heard again and suddenly the
tent flap was whipped open and Vassiliou
plunged inside, barely missing the brewing
kettle. "Eggs, eggs," he said. My first thought
was that he had missed breakfast.

*The Phoenix has been represented in
many forms and in many mediums.*

given by

NIDRAY, Ph

la Institut

Studies

FABULA'S FIREBIRD

The Once and Future Phoenix
Seminar given by Prof. Cole Nidray, Ph.D.
of the Fabula Institute of Ancient Studies

Ubi: Juan Kenobe Lecture Hall
Quando: November 14, 15, 16, 8 p.m.

0258

A Noranda Forest Recycled Papers promotion printed 3 match colours (175 lpi) on 70lb. Stromberg's e-m

Contents

UBI: JUAN KENOBE LECT

QUANDO: NOVEMBER 14,

ATTENDANCE BY INVITATION A

A Noranda Forest Recycled Papers promotion
3 match colours (175 lpi) on 70lb. Phoenix

Fabula Institute Promotion

Design Firm
Eskind Wadell

Art Director
Roslyn Eskind/Malcolm Waddell

Designer
Nicola Lyon

Photographer
The Image Bank (Stock Photo)

Illustrator
Maggie Cash

Client
**Noranda Forest
Recycled Papers**

Copy
Alan Fawcett

Printer
Grafo Printing

Noranda Forest is one of the premier environmental paper manufacturers in Canada. It employs ecologically sound manufacturing processes from the beginning to end of the paper-making process. The papers used on this spread and the following page contain 10% post-consumer waste with a total of 50% recycled fiber.

**Noranda Forest
Recycled Paper Inserts**

Design Firm
Eskind Wadell

Designer
Roslyn Eskind

Illustrator
Kim La Fave

Client
**Noranda Forest
Recycled Papers**

Copy
John Bowles (1)
Alan Fawcett (2,3)

Printer
Baker, Guerney & McClaren

**Noranda Forest Recycled
Papers Promotional Material**

Design Firm
Eskind Wadell

Art Director
Roslyn Eskind

Designer
**Roslyn Eskind,
Nicola Lyon**

Illustrator
Kim La Fave

Client
**Noranda Forest
Recycled Papers**

Printer
Baker, Guerney & McClaren

Safety Calendar

Design Firm
Peat Jariya Design

Art Director/Designer
Peat Jariya

Illustrator
Pool Energy Services' Children

Client
Pool Energy Service Co.

Printer
Boehm

The calendar is printed on recycled paper.

Mires Design
Moving Announcement

Design Firm
Mires Design

Art Director/Designer
José Serrano

Photographer
Chris Wimpey

Copy
Kelley Smothermon

Printer
Bordeax Printers

The firm wanted to announce their move with a "packing-up" approach, so they used recycled cardboard and packing tape for the envelopes.

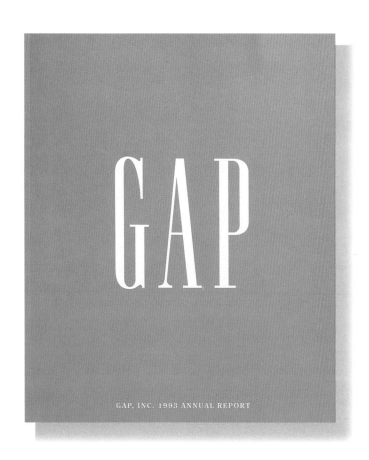

Gap, Inc. 1993 Annual Report

Design Firm
Gap Advertising

Creative Director
Maggie Gross

Designer
Alexis MacDonald

Photographer
Various

Client
Gap, Inc.

Copy
Timothy Cohrs

Print Production Manager
Connie Dorman

Printer
George Rice & Sons

The cover and the financial section uses Nenah Environment which is 100% recycled with 15% post-consumer waste. The remainder uses Crane Classic Crest, which contains 60% recycled fiber with 30% post-consumer. It is printed with soy-based inks and no metallics.

ALL DIVISIONS OF GAP, INC. have demonstrated both the importance of their brand and the rewards of managing it properly. It takes a great deal of time, effort, and money to establish a brand and to engender brand loyalty. And like every vital thing, the Company's brands need constant attention and care to keep them growing. New fabrics, new colors, new patterns, and a constant focus on quality and customers' expectations are crucial elements that the Company addresses on a daily basis. As a result, the Gap brand has grown over the years to become the second largest apparel brand in the world when measured by unit sales.

Advertising and in-store visual merchandising project the image of each of the Company's brands to its target customers. Both are used to announce shifts, such as increased emphasis on women's merchandise, and to herald new deliveries and changes in color palette. Award-winning advertising that continually renews itself, plus windows and in-store displays that change on a semi-weekly basis, keep the Company's brands fresh, vital, and attractive to new and repeat customers alike.

**The Progressive Corporation
1993 Annual Report**

Design Firm
Nesnadny + Schwartz

Art Director
**Mark Schwartz,
Joyce Nesnadny**

Designer
**Joyce Nesnadny, Michelle
Moelher, Mark Schwartz**

Photographer
Zeke Berman

Illustrator
Lavy/Merriam-Webster, Inc.

Client
The Progressive Corporation

Copywriter
**Peter B. Lewis/
The Progressive Corporation**

Printer
Fortran Printing, Inc.

**Recycled paper is used through-
out the book, which is bound
with recycled glue.**

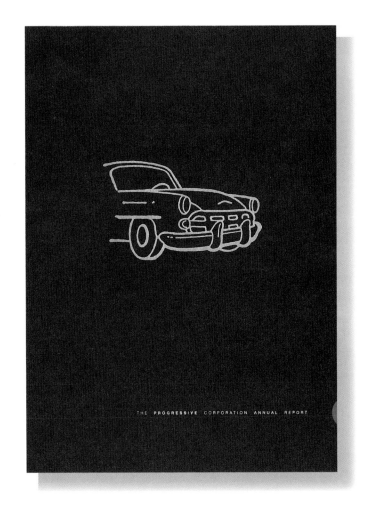

Financial   Highlights   2 · 3

(millions—except per share amounts)

				Average Annual Compounded Rate of Increase (Decrease)	
For the Year	**1993**	**1992**	**% Change**	**1989-1993**	**1984-1993**
Direct premiums written	$ 1,966.4	$ 1,636.8	20	8	23
Net premiums written	1,819.2	1,451.2	25	7	22
Net premiums earned	1,668.7	1,426.1	17	7	21
Total revenues	1,954.8	1,738.9	12	8	22
Income before cumulative effect of accounting change	267.3	139.6	91	20	28
Net income	267.3	153.8	74	20	26
Per share:					
Income before cumulative effect of accounting change	3.58	1.85	94	24	28
Net income	3.58	2.05	75	24	26
Underwriting margin	10.7%	3.5%			
At Year-end					
Consolidated shareholders' equity	$ 997.9	$ 629.0	59	19	29
Common Shares outstanding	72.1	67.1	7	(2)	—
Book Value per Common Share	$ 12.62	$ 7.94	59	20	27
Return on average shareholders' equity	36.0%	34.7%			
Stock Price Appreciation[1]	**1-Year**			**5-Year**	**10-Year**
Progressive	39.8%			40.7%	28.2%
S&P 500	10.1%			14.6%	14.9%

[1]Assumes dividend reinvestment.

Wheels Triptych 1994

**Cleveland Institute of Art
Catalog**

Design Firm
Nesnadny + Schwartz

Art Director
Mark Schwartz, Joyce Nesnadny

Designer
Joyce Nesnadny, Brian Lavy

Photographer
Robert Muller, Mark Schwartz

Client
Cleveland Institute of Art

Copywriter
Anne Brooks Ranallo

Printer
Fortran Printing, Inc.

**Recycled paper and soy-based
inks are used throughout.
Recycled glue is used for
the perfect binding.**

134

Painting. Painting students learn the theory and practice of painti
whose works have been exhibited and collected throughout the US
Their individual studios are well designed for them to observe the
learn how to respond to diverse ideas and forms through one-on-c
define and express their own ideas, rather than be limited by an
museum and a large contemporary art center allows students to co
climate of painting. It also challenges their aesthetic sense and g
community of painters. Other catalysts for students' growth are vis
painting students with British art schools.   Our thorough attent
perception that are needed in pragmatic fields. Painting graduates f
tion, operation of galleries and museums, and as practicing, exhibit

pAi Nt iN g

We stimulate aspiring artists to confront their individual creative powe For our world of intense competition and rapid change, we prepare indivic als with confidence, self-reliance, integrity, and responsibility. Julian Stancz

By teaching both perceptual and conceptual approaches, we aim for a comprehensive understanding of painting — one that is intellectual, physical, and intuitive. Kenneth Dingwall

dely experienced faculty of committed painters
Painting students also learn from one another.
ach other's work, to exchange attitudes, and to
and group critiques. We encourage students to
trend. CIA's proximity to a world-class art
date their knowledge of the history and current
eling of belonging to an ancient and ongoing
guished artists and a new program to exchange
tudent leads to the self-discipline and depth of
ed in graduate school, teaching, art administra-

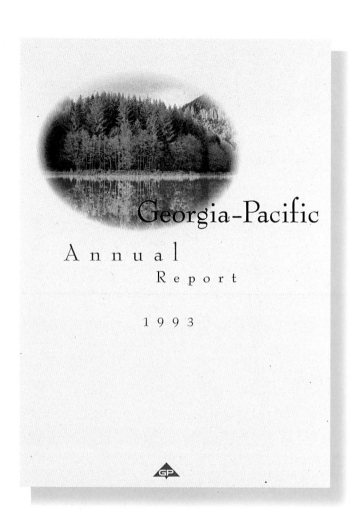

Georgia Pacific Annual Report

Design Firm
Samata Associates

Art Director
Jim Hardy

Designer
Jim Hardy, Susan Mechniq

Photographer
Marc Norberg

Illustrator
John Youssi

Client
Georgia Pacific

Copy
Steve Huggins

Printer
George Rice & Sons

Production/Printing
4-color process, PMS, O/A Dull Varnish

All printed on recycled paper from Georgia Pacific forest land—an area that is reforested specifically to grow trees for paper. The book reflects Georgia Pacific's respect and concern for the renewal process.

increased per capita paper consumption in export markets is expected to boost market pulp demand. Georgia-Pacific exports approximately 65 percent of its market pulp, and operates pulp sales offices in France, Germany, Hong Kong, Italy, Japan, Switzerland, Taiwan and the United Kingdom. ◆ A conversion project at G-P's Brunswick, Georgia, pulp mill in the first half of 1993 expanded the company's production of fluff pulp to approximately 550 thousand tons per year. Fluff pulp is used primarily in disposable diapers and other sanitary items. These products are experiencing growing demand, particularly in developing countries. ◆ Market pulp prices in 1993 were lower than in 1992. Weak economies in major export markets—especially Japan and Western Europe—reduced demand, and changes in currency exchange rates increased the relative cost of U.S.-produced market pulp. Although a number of noncompetitive market pulp mills closed in 1993 and more are expected to close in 1994, world capacity is expected to increase approximately 2 percent in both 1994 and 1995. A significant rebound in pulp prices will likely require economic recoveries in the major importing countries.

TISSUE   Georgia-Pacific is the fifth-largest producer of tissue in the United States, with approximately 9 percent of the industry's capacity. We annually manufacture over 500 thousand tons of tissue at 5 mills. Consumer and commercial tissue products made at our 6 converting facilities include paper towels, napkins and bath tissue. ◆ We sell most of our consumer products under our brand names Angel Soft,® Sparkle,® Coronet,® MD® and Delta® through major retailers of food and general merchandise. G-P also produces commercial tissue products for industrial, food-service, office, hotel, motel and hospital markets. ◆ Tissue demand tends to be relatively stable through economic cycles. Competition in the industry is intense. Improved tissue margins in 1993 resulted from increased volume, higher prices and lower costs.

Environmental
Stewardship
is more than a
responsibility; it is a
necessity. Timberlands
cover one-third of America
and shelter us all. As one of
the United States' leading
forest products companies,
Georgia-Pacific recognizes and readily
accepts the challenge of sustaining a
proper balance of nature and need.
Our land, air and water are renewable only
if we respect them as vital natural resources.
Farmers of a renewable resource must also be
stewards of the land; ours is a business based
on future generations.

Impressions of Hagley

Hagley Museum and Library
Annual Report

Design Firm
Michael Gunselman, Inc.

All Design
Michael Gunselman

Photographer
Michael Kane, Charles Foote

Client
Hagley Museum and Library

Copywriter
Jill A. MacKenzie, Glenn Porter

Printer
Schmitz Press

The cover and inside text are
both printed on recycled paper.

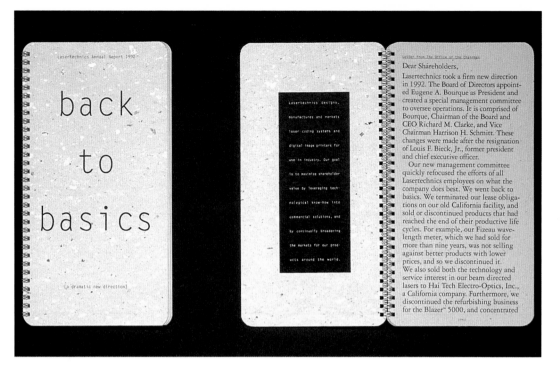

Back to Basics

Design Firm
Vaughn Wedeen Creative

Art Director
Steve Wedeen

Designer
Steve Wedeen

Client
Lasertechnics, Inc.

Copywriter
Nathan James, Steve Wedeen

Printer
Prisma Graphic

The book uses various recycled stocks, including French Dur-O-Tone, French Speckletone, and Simpson LaMonte, as well as basketweave and safety paper.

Croatia Fundraiser

Design Firm
Mires Design, Inc.

Art Director
Scott Mires

Designer
Scott Mires

Illustrator
Gerald Bustamante

Client
Anuska Smith

Copywriter
Anuska Smith

Printer
Graphics Ink

Production/Printing
One-color printing on recycled Kraft paper

The design is simple and not too flashy or "slick" because the designers did not want to detract from the main focus of the event, which was to raise funds for the victims of the Croatian war.

**Warner Bros. proudly presents
"Holiday Favorites"**

Design Firm
Modern Dog

Art Director
Jeri Heiden

Designer
**Robynne Raye,
Michael Strassburger**

Illustrator
Robynne Raye

Client
Warner Brothers Records

Copywriter
**Robynne Raye, Anna McAllister,
and recording superstars**

Whenever possible, Modern Dog tries to think beyond just using recycled paper and soy-based inks. When Warner Bros. asked them to design a Christmas card, the firm wanted to create a design piece that didn't end up in the garbage after the Holidays. By creating a mini cookbook full of recipes from their roster of recording stars, they developed a piece that people will hold on to.

RIGGS BANK

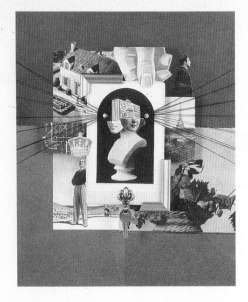

ITS MØRE THAN MØNEY
its your future

ANACHRØBØTICA

GØDDESS ØF ILLUSTRATIØN

STYLE MAGAZINE

SHØPPING'S BRAVE NEW WØRLD

ASTD

RACISM & DIVERSITY
trading places at monsanto

Pat Hackett Christmas Card

Design Firm
The Leonhardt Group

Art Director
Janet Kruse

Designer
Janet Kruse, Traci Daberko

Client
**Pat Hackett, Artist
Representative**

Copywriter
Jeff Fraga

Printer
**Bridge Town, Copy Company,
and Aculine**

The intent of the project was to create a collector's item that no one would want to throw away. The cover of the box is covered with 100% post-consumer recycled paper and the cards inside are wrapped in tissue paper.

E.W. Media Planning Guide

Design Firm
Platinum Design, Inc.

Art Director
Peslak/Quinn

Designer
Quinn

Illustrator
Sergio Baradot

Client
Entertainment Weekly

Printer
Enterprise Press

The entire media guide is printed on recycled paper.

David Plunkert Self Promo
(facing page)

Art Director/Designer
David Plunkert

The cards are printed 4-color process on recycled paper.

141

BLOWN
AWAY

Blown Away

Design Firm
Mike Salisbury Communications

Art Director
Tami Masuda

Designer
**Mike Salisbury,
Patrick O'Neal**

Client
MGM

Printer
Gore Graphics

Production/Printing
Offset

**Since few motion pictures
are promoted with books,
the designer wanted to be as
environmentally conscious
as possible. The entire catalog
is printed on recycled paper
with soy-based inks.**

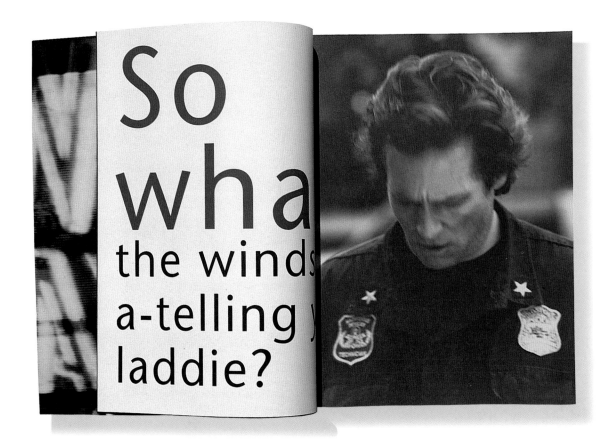

So wha the winds a-telling y laddie?

Social Stationery

Design Firm
Michael Mabry Design

Art Director
Mitch Nash

Designer
Michael Mabry

Illustrator
Michael Mabry

Client
Blue Q

Copywriter
Michael Mabry

Printer
**Quality Printing (letterheads),
Andrews Printing (box
& packet wraps)**

This "Social Stationery"
includes recyclable die-cut corrugated boxes and is printed on
100% recycled French paper.

**Cathay Pacific/Cuisine
from the Land Down Under
Inflight Menus**

Design Firm
PPA Design Limited

Art Director
Byron Jacobs

Designer
Byron Jacobs

Client
Cathay Pacific Airways

Copywriter
Joanne Jones

Printer
Ching Luen Printing

Production/Printing
4-color offset and letterpress

This Australian food promotion
centers around Chef Scot
Webster's cuisine. It is produced
with a simple binding and
recycled stock to be completely
biodegradable if thrown away.

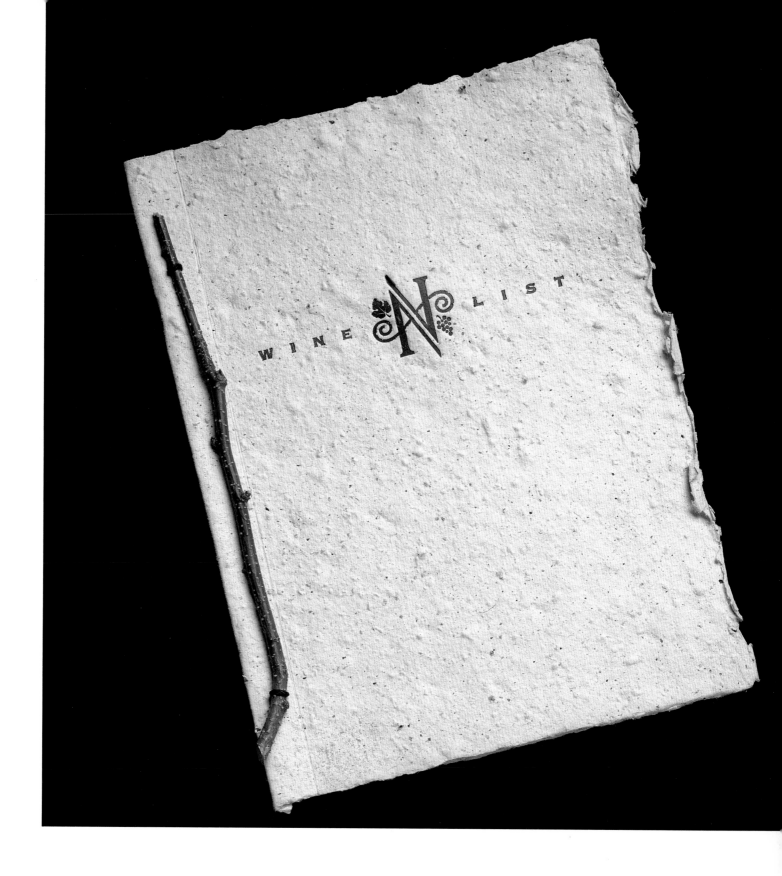

Napa Valley Grille
Wine List Cover

Design Firm
Tharp Did It

Art Director
Rick Tharp

Designer
Rick Tharp, Colleen Sullivan

Client
California Cafe Restaurant Corp.

Printer
Evanescent Press

This hand-bound letter-pressed
wine list is constructed from
handmade paper consisting of
natural fibers and the juice,
seeds, and skins of grapes. It is
bound with a grapevine stem.

THE COMMUNITY CHEST
OF HONG KONG
TWENTY SECOND
ANNUAL REPORT 1990/91
香港公益金第二十二期年報
一九九〇至九一年度

Mohawk Display System
(facing page)

Design Firm
Pentagram Design/NY

Art Director
**Michael Zechbrenner,
Jim Bieber**

Client
Mohawk Paper Mills, Inc.

This system is used for receptions and trade shows and highlights Mohawk's identity and packaging by using the actual web roll-wrap to cover the table, chair, and lamps. All of the pieces break down to fit into a shipping crate. This makes an attractive display, but also eliminates the need for expensive, non-biodegradable materials to build the booth. No cleaning chemicals are needed either, since the wrap is disposable but recyclable.

爲善最樂 福有攸歸

**The Community Chest
of Hong Kong
Twenty Second Annual Report**

Design Firm
**Kan Tài-keung Design &
Associates, Ltd.**

Art Director
**Kan Tài-keung/
Eddy Yu Chi Kong**

Designer
**Eddy Yu Chi Kong/Joyce Hó
Ngai Sing**

Photographer
Franklin Lau

Client
**The Community Chest
of Hong Kong**

The center image on the work is a Chinese New Year motif meaning "happiness." The Chinese character is made up of objects and photographs relevant to each of the services mentioned in the brochure. The entire piece is printed on recycled paper.

Medox Display Series

Design Firm
Mike Quon Design Office

Art Director
Nancy Artino

Designer
Mike Quon

Illustrator
Mike Quon

Client
Medox

This series of displays/posters
are targeted to vascular sur-
geons. They are printed in six
colors on recycled Curtis
Tweedweave 65# cover.

**Deleo Clay Tile
Calendar**
(facing page, bottom)

Design Firm
Mires Design, Inc.

Art Director
José Serrano, Scott Mires

Designer
José Serrano, Scott Mires

Photographer
Chris Wimpey

Client
Deleo Clay Tile Company

Printer
Rush Press

As with all Deleo materials,
the calendar is printed on
recycled paper.

**Vaughn Wedeen Creative
10th Anniversary Invitation**

Design Firm
Vaughn Wedeen Creative

Art Director
Steve Wedeen, Rick Vaughn

Designer
Rick Vaughn

Illustrator
Rick Vaughn

Copywriter
**Richard Kuhn, Nathan James,
Steve Wedeen, Rick Vaughn**

Printer
Weldy Silkscreen

This 11-page invitation/promo
book was screen printed on
chipboard and then die-cut.
Chipboard is one of the most
rudimentary recycled stocks—
most printers use it for
packing applications.

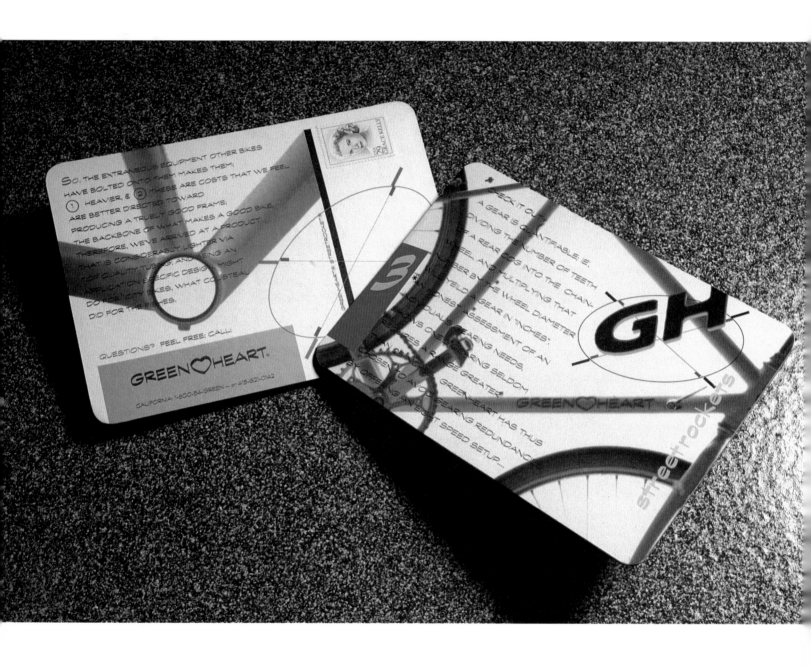

So, the extraneous equipment other bikes have bolted onto them makes them; ① heavier, & ② these are costs that we feel are better directed toward producing a truely good frame; the backbone of what makes a good bike. Therefore, we've arrived at a product that is considerably lighter via top quality tubing; and, being an application specific design, might do for city bikes, what Cousteau did for the fishes.

Questions? Feel free; call!

GREEN♥HEART.

California: 1-800-54-GREEN — or 415-821-0142

Check it out: a gear is quantifiable, ie. dividing the number of teeth of a rear cog into the chain-wheel, and multiplying that number by the wheel diameter ... yields a gear in "inches". ... dual assessment of an ... individual's own gearing needs, ... range seldom ... or range greater ... Green♥heart has thus ... greening an ... speed setup ...

GH

GREEN♥HEART

streetrockets

Greenheart
"Street Rocket" Series

Design Firm
Barbara Ziller &
Associates Design

Art Director
Barbara Ziller, Andrew Graef

Designer
Andrew Graef, Barbara Ziller

Photographer
Kevin Sanchez

Client
Greenheart Design

Copywriter
Andrew Graef

Printer
Blacksheep Press

Production/Printing
4-color Litho and Silk screen

The lamination to E Flute was
a jump from a flat sheet to a
more tactile object. The recyclable postcard eliminates the
need for a separate envelope.
The objective was to attract,
on a very limited budget, an
audience interested in environmentally friendly products.

Vote, gripe, complain, bitch, moan, groan, whine, curse, reject, refuse, neglect, grouch, grumble, protest, procrastinate, postpone, denounce, defend, ignore, deplore...

It's time to stop talking and do something. Like participate. And vote.

The annual election of the communicating arts group board of directors will be held thursday november 19 at tomato's (3111 sports arena blvd). Talk starts at 6. Food (good italian stuff) at 7. Guest speaker bob kwait (award-winning zoo guy) at 7:45. Election at 8:15. Members pay $12. Non members $15. (People who make a reservation and don't show will be billed.) If you can't make it then (at least) send in the proxy ballot. Mark 3 choices or write in some different ones:

○ frank cleaver (vp fine arts store) ○ rebecca debreau (graphic design, m.c.w.e.)
○ diane ditucci (sales, arts and crafts press) ○ elyce ellington (graphics manager, m.c.w.e.)
○ laura koonce-jose (computer production, quorum) ○ linda lampman (art director, lambesis communications) ○ tom okerlund (copywriter/art director, kpbs-tv) ○ someone (anyone) else: _____. Sign your name here _____ and mail to cag (3108 5th ave suite f san diego 92103) by november 17 or fax (295-3822) by november 19.

Vote

Design Firm
Mires Design, Inc.

Art Director
John Ball

Designer
John Ball

Illustrator
David Quattrociocchi

Client
Communicating Arts Group

Printer
Graphics Ink

This promotional mailer was printed on recycled Simpson Evergreen Birch paper.

**Hermann Hospital
Christmas Card**

Design Firm
Peat Jariya Design

Art Director/Designer
Peat Jariya

Photographer
Steve Chenn Photography

Client
Hermann Hospital

Production
4-color process, foil stamp

Recycled paper gives these
cards a rich texture.

**[Metal] General
Occasion Cards**

Design Firm
Peat Jariya Design

Art Director
Peat Jariya

Designer
Peat Jariya, Terry Asker

Photographer
Terry Asker Photography

Client
[Metal] Studio Corp.

Production
4-color process

General occasion cards printed
on soft recycled paper preserve
the quality and beauty of hand-
transferred photography.

Tree Card

Design Firm
Dewitt Kendall

Art Director
DeWitt Kendall

Printer
Leitch Printing Corp.

Printed on recycled paper (Simpson Gainsborough) the tree card is sold and distributed as a bereavement note card. The card was printed on what otherwise would have been a wasted piece of press sheet from another job. The custom-converted envelope is made from recycled brown Kraft paper that has not been de-inked.

Wedding Invitation

Design Firm
J. Graham Hanson Graphic Design

Art Director/Designer
J. Graham Hanson

Client
Owens/Hanson Wedding

Printer
Purgatory Pie Press

The invitation was printed on recycled Simpson Evergreen and bound with natural Japanese fiber. It was printed on a letterpress, eliminating the need for harsh chemicals to develop offset plates. The binding sticks were gathered in New York City's Central Park.

Goose Island Menu

Design Firm
Petrick Design

Art Director/Designer
Robert Petrick

Client
Goose Island Brewing Company

This menu is created from corrugated cardboard that is split to make its own binding. The menu is updated by gluing new sheets into the recycled shells.

Alternatives
875 6th Avenue
26th Floor
New York, NY 10001
212-239-0600

American Recordings
3500 West Olive #1550
Burbank, CA 91505
818-973-4545

Barbara Ziller
& Associates Design
330 Fell Street
San Francisco, CA 94102
415-621-0330

Burkur Design Group
865 N. LaSalle
Chicago, IL 60610
312-440-0240

CAW
Pfingstanger 19
31191 Algermissen
Germany
1149-5126-8660

Cato Gobe & Associates
411 Lafayette Street
2nd Floor
New York, NY 10003
212-979-8900

Clifford Selbert Design
2067 Massachusetts Avenue
Cambridge, MA 02140
617-497-6605

Cornerstone
444 Park Avenue South
New York, NY 10016
212-686-6046

Design Guys
119 North Fourth Street
Suite 410
Minneapolis, MN 55401
612-338-4462

Design Factory
3+4 Merrion Place
Dublin 2, Ireland
353-1-6612600

Design House Consultants
120 Parkway
London NW1 7AN
England
021-482-2815

DeWitt Kendall
5000 Marine Drive 4D
Chicago, IL 60640
312-275-7884

Earl Gee Design
501 Second Street
Suite 700
San Francisco, CA 94107
415-543-1192

Eric Baker
Design Associates, Inc.
156 5th Avenue
New York, NY 10010
212-463-7094

Eskind Wadell
260 Richmond Street West
Suite 201
Toronto, Ontario
M5V 1WS Canada
416-593-1626

Fitch, Inc.
10350 Olentangy River Road
Columbus, OH 43085
614-885-3453

Gap Advertising
2 Harrison Street
San Francisco, CA 94105
415-952-4400

Geffen Records
9130 Sunset
Los Angeles, CA 90069
310-285-2781

Grafik Communications Ltd.
1199 N. Fairfax Street
Suite 700
Alexandria, VA 22314
703-683-4686

Hanson Associates, Inc.
133 Grape Street
Philadelphia, PA 19127
215-487-7051

Holden & Co.
804 College Avenue
Santa Rosa, CA 95404
707-575-4462

Hollywood Records
500 South Buena Vista Street
Burbank, CA 91521
818-560-5795

Horner/Rundquist, Inc.
1800 Century Boulevard
Suite 1225
Atlanta, GA 30345
404-321-0023

Independent Project Press
Box 1033
Sedona, AZ 86339
602-204-1332

J. Graham Hanson
Graphic Design
307 East 89th Street No. 6G
New York, NY 10128
212-348-8078

Jager DiPaola Kemp Design
308 Pine Street
Burlington, VT 05401
802-864-5884

John Gamble Graphic Design
341 Crown Street
New Haven, CT 06511
203-562-3551

Joseph Rattan Design
4445 Travis #104
Dallas, TX 95205
214-520-3180

Kan Tai-keung Design &
Associates, Ltd.
28/F Great Smart Tower
230 Wanchai Road
Hong Kong
852-574-8399

Lebowitz/Gould/Design, Inc.
7W 22 Street
New York, NY 10010
212-645-0550

The Leonhardt Group
1218 3rd Avenue No. 620
Seattle, WA 98101
206-624-0551

Leslie Chan Design Co., Ltd.
47, 115 Nanking E. Road Sec 4
Taipei Taiwan
02-545-5435

Little & Company
1010 S. 7th Street
Minneapolis, MN 55415
612-375-0077

Luis Fitch Diseno
4104 Pinetree Drive
10th Floor #1031
Miami Beach, FL 33140

Maurizio di Robilant & Associates
via Lamarmora 36
20122 Milano Italy
39-2-5518-4817

Michael Gunselman, Inc.
1400 North Franklin Street
Wilmington, DE 19806
302-655-7077

Michael Mabry Design
212 Sutter Street
San Francisco, CA 94108
415-982-7336

Michael Schwab Design
80 Liberty Ship Way #7
Saulsalito, CA 94965
415-331-7621

Mike Quon Design Office
568 Broadway #703
New York, NY 10012
212-226-6024

Mike Salisbury Communications
2200 Amapola Court
Torrance, CA 90501
310-320-7660

Mires Design, Inc.
2345 Kettner Boulevard
San Diego, CA 92101
619-234-6631

Modern Dog
601 Valley Street
No. 309
Seattle, WA 98109
206-282-8857

Morla Design
463 Bryant Street
San Francisco, CA 94107
415-543-6548

Nesnadny + Schwartz
10803 Magnolia Drive
Cleveland, OH 44106
216-791-7721

Nippon Design Center, Inc.
1-13-13 Ginza, Chuo-ku
Tokyo, 104, Japan
03-3567-3232

One World Solutions Inc.
220 West 19 Street
New York, NY 10011
212-989-5440

Paper Shrine
604 France Street
Baton Rouge, LA 70802
504-346-6779

Petrick Design
828 N. Walcott Avenue
Chicago, IL 60622
312-486-2880

Peat Jariya Design
13164 Memorial Drive #222
Houston, TX 77079
713-523-5175

Pentagram Design/NY
212 5th Avenue
17th Floor
New York, NY 10010
212-683-7000

Peterson & Company
2200 N. Lamar Suite 310
Dallas, TX 75202
214-954-0522

Planet Design Company
229 State Street
Madison, WI 53703
608-256-0000

Platunum Design, Inc.
14 W. 23 Street
New York, NY 10010
212-366-4000

Plunkert, David
3647 Falls Rd.
Baltimore, MD 21211
410-235-7803

PPA Design Limited
D-3, 11 MacDonnell Road
Midlevels, Hong Kong
852-810-6640

The Pushpin Group
215 Park Avenue S. #1300
New York, NY 10003
212-674-8080

Richardson or Richardson
1301 East Bethany Home Road
Phoenix, AZ 85014
602-266-1301

Rigelhaupt Design
18 East 16th Street
4th Floor
New York, NY 10003
212-206-9141

Samata Associates
101 South First Street
Dundee, IL 60118
708-428-8600

Segura Inc.
361 West Chestnut Street
1st Floor
Chicago, IL 60610
312-649-5688

Sibley/Peteet Design, Inc.
965 Slocum
Dallas, TX 75207
214-761-9400

J. Otto Seibold
38 W. 21st Street #1101
New York, NY 10010
212-366-4949

Sommese Design
481 Glenn Road
State College, PA 16803
814-238-7484

Stoltze Design
49 Melcher Street
Boston, MA 02210
617-350-7109

Tharp Did It
50 University Avenue
Suite 21
Los Gatos, CA 95030
408-354-6726

Thom & Dave Marketing Design, Inc.
28 West State Street
Media, PA 19063
610-566-0566

Trickett & Webb
The Factory
84 Marchmont Street
London WC1N 1HE England
071-388-5832

UCI Inc.
3660 Waialae Avenue
Suite 207
Honolulu, HI 96816

Vaughn Wedeen Creative
407 Rio Grande Blvd. NW
Albuquerque, NM 87104
505-243-4000

Warner Bros. Records
3300 Warner Boulevard
Burbank, CA 91505
818-953-3361

Weber Design Partners, Inc.
1439 Larimer Square
Denver, CO 80202
303-892-9816

Werner Design Werks
126 N. 3rd Street #400
Minneapolis, MN 55401
612-338-2550